Report of War Department Equipment Board, Part 1

Combined Arms Research Library

SECRET

REPORT OF

WAR DEPARTMENT

EQUICMENT BOARD

See DA Circular 310-21 dated
17 Oct 57 which regrade report
dated 29 May 46

SECRET

WDGDS   **9758**   20 February 1946

MEMORANDUM FOR THE COMMANDANT, COMMAND AND GENERAL STAFF SCHOOL
FORT LEAVENWORTH, KANSAS

SUBJECT: Report of War Department Equipment Board (Stilwell Board)

     1.   Attached hereto is a copy of the Report of the War Department
Equipment Board, dated 19 January 1946.

     2.   It is desired that interested divisions of your Staff (or Technical
Services) review the report and submit comments and recommendations to this
office.   These recommendations should include the part or parts of the report
that should be approved, modified, or disapproved.

     3.   It is further desired that recommendations be in this office on or
before 9 March 1946.

        FOR THE ASSISTANT CHIEF OF STAFF, G-4:

1 Incl   JOHN D. BILLINGSLEY
   Rpt of WD Equip Bd   Colonel, GSC
   (Cy No. 16)   Chief, Program Branch

WDGDS 9758   1st Ind

C&GS Sch, Fort Leavenworth, Kansas, 21 March 1946

TO: Assistant Chief of Staff, G-4, War Department General Staff,
Washington, D. C. ATTENTION: Chief, Program Branch

     Comments and recommendations requested in basic letter are furnished
as follows:

     1. Recommend Section IV, paragraphs 12 and 15 be changed to read as
follows:

          a. Par 12. "Communication Equipment. In forward areas, radio
is a vital necessity in communication, as the efficiency of artillery
support will often be dependent upon it. Until radio communication in
forward areas becomes absolutely reliable, the development of wire and
telephone equipment should be given prime importance instead of being
relegated to a secondary role.

          "The use of teletypes down to at least a corps artillery fire
direction center level should be a subject for further improvement in the
compactness and efficiency of teletypewriter sets.

          "Experimentation should be conducted into the possibility of
use of director-type equipment, of size to conform to field artillery
mobility demands, which would permit electrical transmission of firing
data and automatic laying of the weapons. Such a plan is visionary at
the present, but would appear worthy of intense research in order to eliminate the human error as far as possible. In combination with radar
target detection equipment, this automatic laying of weapons would result
in speedier, more effective fire, especially counterbattery and counter-
mortar fire."

          b. Par 15. "The observing instruments available to the field
artillery should be improved with a view to increased magnification and
decreased weight. Battlefield observation should detect more detailed
intelligence than present equipment permits. This applies to air, as
well as ground observers."

     2. Recommend that the following additional items be included in
Section VII:

          a. Development of technique and equipment for construction of
roads and airfields over very deep snow.

          b. Development of standard designs for construction of shelters,
hospitals, military pipelines, and other necessary military installations
in extremely cold climates.

c. Development of landing strip design suitable for ultra high speed aircraft without the conventional wheel-type landing gear.

d. Development of sturdy, compact, simple, light-weight set of navigation instruments for use by ground troops in the arctic.

3. Recommend that Section X, Airborne Equipment, contain a reference to airplane spray tanks and to bombs for screening landing operations.

4. Recommend that Section XII CWS emphasize the remarks made in paragraphs 27, 28 and 29, Section XVI Ammunition.

5. The following comments are offered reference Sections XVII and XIX:

a. Add after paragraph 5 on page 83, and after paragraph 4 on page 98:

"Write into equipment specifications the following:

(1) The bulk of the commonly used signal equipment should be susceptible of skilled use by personnel of not over second year high school level.

(2) Signal equipment should be so designed that operating and using personnel can be trained in its combat use in not to exceed 10 days.

(3) Command post signal equipment assemblies should be provided at all training centers and especially where commanders, general staff and special staff officers are trained. These assemblies should be highly mobile and readily adapted to linkage with similar assemblies representing other command posts. The purpose is to instruct in uniform signal operating procedures, and in sound appreciation of signal capabilities, limitations and in signal security."

b. Add after paragraph 32 on page 90:

"Messenger equipment should be listed on specific development projects. The most efficient means of transportation by air, ground and water should be studied. More effective means are needed for quick message destruction when capture of messenger is imminent."

c. General:

(1) Appendix I should be broken down by activities in addition to alphabetic listing of names.

(2) Stress the necessity for close coordination between the military development board and the civilian manufacturing agencies.

(3) Comments of the various arms and services concerning signal and radar equipment might well have been repeated and coordinated in Sections XVII and XIX.

(4) Establish centrally in the United States underground development, manufacturing and storage facilities.

(5) Emphasize development of long range radio and radar devices, and other signal equipment with their housing and transportation, which are operable in polar areas or under extreme cold conditions.

6. Recommend the following modifications in Section XVIII:

   a. Change paragraph 5 f (6) to read:

   "Transmitting by television a view of the combat area by day or by night."

   b. Change last sentence of paragraph 7 b to read:

   "In addition, further research should be accomplished on means of producing visual images of thermal scenes by means of far infra-red radiation; on means of electronically transposing thermal scenes by means of inherent infra-red radiations from the infra-red into the visible spectrum for examination, photographing or televising, and on means of amplifying the illumination from the night sky."

7. The following additions to paragraph 13, Section XXI, are recommended:

   Types of this equipment should also be designed so as to be readily installed in, or transported by, cargo planes for the servicing of isolated units.

   Accessories should be provided for the laundry and bath units so as to permit the cleansing and re-use of water when these units are operating in areas where there is a scarcity of water.

Incl w/d

O. P. WEYLAND
Major General, USA
Assistant Commandant

REPORT OF

WAR DEPARTMENT

EQUIPMENT BOARD

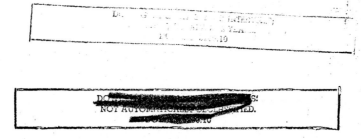

WAR DEPARTMENT
The Adjutant General's Office
Washington 25, D.C.

RHO jch 2303
Off Br-RHC Ph 78270

AG 334 War Dept Equip Board
(4 Oct 45)

8 October 1945

CORRECTED COPY

SUBJECT: Appointment of War Department Equipment Board

TO: Each officer concerned.
2D949 The Pentagon
Washington 25, D. C.

1. A board to be known as the War Department Equipment Board consisting of:

        General Joseph W. Stilwell, 01912, USA, President
        Lieutenant General Lewis H. Brereton, 03132, USA
        Lieutenant General Edmund B. Gregory, 01924, USA
        Lieutenant General Alvan C. Gillem, Jr., 03030, USA
        Brigadier General Clyde C. Alexander, 05974, USA, Recorder

is appointed to meet on or about 1 November 1945 for the purpose of reviewing types of equipment required for the Army Ground Forces in the post-War Army including that equipment used by the Army Air Forces in direct support of ground operations and that equipment for service type units normally a part of a field army.

2. Recommendations of the Board should include the general military characteristics of equipment to be developed and such other matters as the Board deems pertinent and necessary for guidance in developing equipment for the post-War Army.

3. The Army Ground Forces Equipment Review Board Report with remarks and recommendations thereon by the theaters and major commands and other reports that may be referred to the Board by this office will be considered.

4. The Board will report to the Chief of Staff and is authorized to call upon any agency of the War Department or any of its subordinate commands for information and assistance. The members of the Equipment Review Committee will remain available to assist during the Board deliberations.

5. Upon submission of the Board report in quintuple to the Chief of Staff, the Board is dissolved.

BY ORDER OF THE SECRETARY OF WAR:

(OFFICIAL -
THE ADJUTANT GENERAL
WAR DEPARTMENT)

/s/ R. H. CHRISTIE

Adjutant General

19 January 1946.

SUBJECT: Report of War Department Equipment Board.

TO: The Chief of Staff, United States Army.

1. Herewith is the Report of the War Department Equipment Board which was convened on 1 November 1945 pursuant to Letter Instructions, War Department, dated 8 October 1945.

2. The Board has reviewed the types of equipment required for the Army Ground Forces in the postwar Army, including that equipment used by the Army Air Forces in direct support of ground operations and that equipment for service type units normally a part of a field army. In accomplishing that mission, full advantage has been taken of the experience and advice of outstanding civilian scientists and industrialists, as well as representatives of the Army, Navy and Marine Corps.

3. Recommendations covering major policies are contained in Part A of the Report. Part B is devoted to the establishment of requirements and general military characteristics for the equipment deemed necessary for use in the postwar Army.

JOSEPH W. STILWELL,
General, USA, President.

LEWIS H. BRERETON,
Lieutenant General, USA.

EDMUND B. GREGORY,
Lieutenant General, USA.

ALVAN C. GILLEM, JR.
Lieutenant General, USA.

CLYDE C. ALEXANDER,
Brigadier General, USA,
Recorder.

Table of Contents

Part A

Part B

Principal Items of Equipment

Appendix I

PART A

SECTION I

FACTORS INFLUENCING EQUIPMENT POLICIES

1. Four factors were predominant in the winning of our last two wars. These were: (1) great wealth of natural resources; (2) vast industrial capacity to turn resources into weapons; (3) space between our shores and the enemy, which gave, (4) time in which to build a military machine. Reliance can no longer be placed on two of these factors, space and time. Another factor, vast industrial capacity, is threatened by the appearance of atomic explosive. Requirements of the past war, involving production of almost countless varieties and quantities of equipment, could not have been met had not our industry functioned at an increasing tempo. Industry was not attacked during that war. In future wars, that condition will not exist.

2. Atomic explosive, nuclear radioactive materials, biological agents and chemical gases promise results on a scale thousands of times greater than that possible with conventional weapons and with a minimum expenditure of men and materiel. It is possible for a small nation, properly directed and equipped with outstanding scientific research facilities, to devastate a larger foe. Since war has become total, fear of retaliation by an opponent more ably equipped to wage total war is the most powerful deterrent. Therefore, this country must be prepared to employ instantly all means and methods for the total destruction of an enemy.

3. Arrival at this stage of warfare, where total destruction of a foe is possible in a very short period of time, makes it imperative that this nation retain its lead in scientific research.

4. In addition to the necessity for scientific research, the proceedings of the Board have revealed the following vitally important items that require immediate consideration:

    a. The power of the atomic bomb, its influence upon strategical concepts, and the necessity for re-evaluation of strategic outlying bases in the light of new concepts.

    b. The catastrophic potentiality of biological and chemical agents and the necessity for providing protective countermeasures for the entire civil population.

    c. The necessity of obtaining continuous information as to the intentions, scientific programs, industrial trends and war potentials of foreign countries.

Research and Development

5. Scientific research is a paramount factor in National Defense. The greatly accelerated pace of research has produced revolutionary developments in the fields of nuclear physics, chemistry and biology. The effect on civilization may well be as great as the discovery of fire. Almost overnight, new and greatly improved means of warfare have become available. Conversely, conventional weapons can be only slightly improved.

6. At the close of the war scientists were on the verge of many new discoveries and improvements in practically all fields of military equipment. They are now turning to their peacetime pursuits. It is mandatory that some procedure be adopted whereby scientific research is accorded a major role in the postwar development of military equipment. The scientific talent available within the military establishment is not adequate for this task and must be augmented.

7. The military establishment, science and industry should be welded together in mutual understanding and cooperation for National Defense by intimate association. In general, the scientific laboratories of the Technical Services should be devoted to those problems so peculiarly military as to have no counterpart among civilian research facilities, meanwhile utilizing, on contract basis, the civilian educational institutions and industrial laboratories for the solution of problems within their scope.

8. Continuous guidance of the research program is essential. Further, the discoveries of independent scientific research must be ascertained and evaluated for possible military application.

9. A long range development program is necessary for the successful guidance of the development of equipment and the research preceding the actual design. However, no one can see far into the future, and the program should be kept flexible. Research may produce at any moment new knowledge that will require a partial, or even complete, adjustment of the program. In general, two parallel courses must be followed: vigorous research and development of the new or anticipated types of equipment, and continued improvement of existing equipment as an interim measure. Therefore, an agency is required to supervise continuously research and development, merging or terminating projects at the feasible, economical moment and assuring a step-by-step change-over from the discarded material or method to the new.

10. Under favorable conditions, a long time is required from the conception of the need for an item of equipment to its development, test, production and delivery on the battlefield. Technical planning and operational planning must go hand in hand. Those responsible for the guidance of the research and development program should be on the same staff level with and participate in all strategical and operational planning in order

2

that needs for new equipment may be determined, and research and development thereof be initiated at the earliest moment.

11. The limitations that will be imposed on funds during the postwar period, and the shortage of research talent in comparison to the multitudinous items requiring further research and development, necessitate most careful selection of the items to which research and development will be devoted. A system of priorities should be established, and maintained currently, whereby an apportionment of available funds is made as between research projects, development projects, and actual procurement of new equipment and whereby within each grouping the priority of the projects is established. Initially, the bulk of funds should be apportioned to research. Priority should be assigned in the following order:

    a. (1) Items that are vitally necessary to meet new
             conditions of warfare.

        (2) Items of such potential importance that their
             value must be determined at the earliest possible moment.

    b. Items of new application which will supplant existing types of equipment.

    c. Newer models of existing types of equipment which demonstrate marked superiority over existing models.

    d. Improvement and modernization of existing models in accordance with advances in technology.

12. The following measures are necessary to implement research and development in the postwar Army:

    a. Establishment of a Directorate of Research and Development as a separate General Staff Division on the Directorate level of the War Department. This Directorate should supersede the New Developments Division of the Special Staff, and extend its scope.

        (1) Personnel. The Director should be a senior general
             officer. For the Research activities, the key personnel should include: one officer from each Arm and Technical Service, each of whom should possess outstanding knowledge of the development of equipment pertaining to his Arm or Service; a nationally known scientist as the senior assistant to the Director, and one outstanding scientist in each major field of

3

science. The civilian personnel should be obtained on a rotation basis from scientific
colleges and industrial laboratories. For the
Development activities, the key personnel should
include general officers drawn from the field
commands of the Arms and Services, and one qualified officer from each Arm and Technical Service.

    (2) <u>Mission</u>. The mission of the Directorate of Research
and Development should specifically include the
following:

        (a) Supervision over all Army research activities,
and formulation of clear, definite military
needs in the field of research, and translation
of those needs into basic and applied research
projects.

        (b) Establishment of priorities of research, and
equitable apportionment of research tasks to
all available research agencies.

        (c) Maintenance of intimate relationship with all
civilian research agencies and the evaluation
of independent civilian research findings for
possible military application.

        (d) Overall supervision of a long range program
for equipping the postwar Army, and continuous
review and evaluation of all development programs, including participation in operational
planning to determine needs for new equipment.

        (e) Analysis of the actual value of, or need for,
an item of equipment, and the establishment of
priorities for development.

        (f) Coordination of that part of the budget pertain-
ing to research and development.

  b. Augmenting scientific talent within the Army and providing for
continuity of talent by:

    (1) Commissioning in the Regular Army, Reserve and National
Guard officers and civilians of outstanding scientific
background.

    (2) Furthering the scientific education of officers and

civilian scientists permanently employed by the
Army, through attendance at educational institutions as students and by means of exchange fellow-
ships arranged with leading universities and industrial laboratories; and by attendance, on a
duty status, at appropriate scientific gatherings.

(3) Selecting members of each graduating class of the
Military Academy for attendance at scientific
colleges, and commissioning each year in the Regu-
lar Army selected graduates of scientific colleges.

c. Making salaries available that will attract the type of civilian
scientist required for key positions in the Directorate of Research and Development.

d. Adoption of the long range program for equipping the postwar
Army presented in Part B of this report.

Principles Applicable to Development of Equipment

13. Research may produce at any moment new knowledge that will require
a complete readjustment of any program of development. For that reason, no
specific recommendation made in this report as to the military characteristics of an item of equipment should be taken as a rigid requirement. Where
specific recommendations are made, the Board is indicating what the next step
in development should be.

14. As development progresses in the field of nuclear energy, or in any
other field where the results are applicable in combat, the using services
should be given sufficient information, consistent with security, to enable
them to make the most efficient use of material and method.

15. Commercial development cannot be expected on items that are not
remunerative or that will upset established trade practices. Military development must ignore financial considerations and be governed only by required
efficiency. Departures from the conventional, therefore, must be encouraged.
This is especially applicable in the case of motor vehicles.

16. Changes in tactics and organization affect the development of weapons
and equipment, since from proposed new tactical uses or organizational group-
ings, demands are created for new equipment. At the same time, research and
development may be capable of supplying a new article but lack the demand to
create it due to the failure of the tactical user to visualize and request
what to him is unknown. The concepts of future tactics, organization and
equipment should be examined and stated clearly in order that research and
development can be directed intelligently.

5

17. The beginning of the war found the Army with equipment predicated on temperate zone and average terrain conditions, with little knowledge of equipment required for global use in extremes of climate and terrain. Insofar as practicable, all equipment should be designed to withstand and operate under extreme conditions of climate and terrain, or to be capable of modification for such operation, with appropriate special equipment available to replace that not capable of global use. Provision should be made for both engineering and troop service tests of equipment in areas corresponding to all climatic and terrain conditions likely to be encountered in future warfare.

18. A force of combined Arms, under specially selected alert and progressive commanders, should be designated to conduct extended service tests of new weapons and equipment. After tests have been conducted by Service Boards and any necessary modifications of the equipment have been made, a sufficient number of weapons, or equipment, should be procured to equip an appropriate unit of the force of combined Arms and to enable tactical employment, doctrine, and allowances to be formulated by practical application in the field.

19. Tables of Organization and Equipment should reflect variable geographical considerations by incorporating therein additional columns of allowances to show clearly the deletions of standard equipment, or modifications to be made thereto, and equipment prescribed in lieu thereof, for desert, tropical-jungle, mountain, and arctic service. Where the changes in equipment involve personnel, that factor should be shown also.

20. War Department policy envisages that the user should indicate the equipment desired, defined in terms of military characteristics, and that the user will maintain close coordination with the developer, including participation during design, mockup, and engineering test phases. That policy is sound and should be pursued vigorously to the end that the field experience of the user and technical skill of the designer are mutually brought to bear in the early solution of any intermediate problems. Coordination of this procedure should be effected by the Director of Research and Development, as indicated in paragraph 12 a.

21. The value of educational orders as a means of informing industry of the development of military weapons and equipment and to facilitate going into production when a necessity arises was clearly demonstrated immediately prior to the outbreak of the recent war. These orders should be continued. In addition, the program of industrial mobilization should be revised in the light of recent war experience. Procurement procedures should be streamlined so that contracts may be awarded with the minimum of delay. In connection with surveys of industrial facilities, stockpiles of critical materials not readily available should be provided in quantities sufficient to at least meet initial industrial mobilization demands.

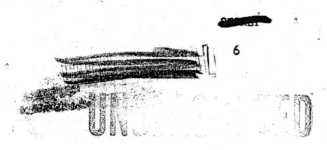

22. a. Equipment of the Infantryman should be reduced in weight and be accorded the highest priority in the allocation of lightweight materials. Insofar as practicable, all infantry weapons and equipment should be capable of being separated into component loads weighing not more than 25 pounds.

b. To keep the number of types of equipment to a minimum, individual and crew served weapons and equipment adopted for Infantry should be prescribed as standard for all other Arms and Services requiring similar equipment.

23. In general, equipment used in the past war exceeded in mechanical performance the ability of the individual to operate it with optimum results in the stress of battle. In many instances, although present technology cannot improve the efficiency of a weapon by more than ten to twenty percent, thorough training carried to perfection could attain increased efficiency of from thirty to fifty percent in the use of the weapon. Therefore, training data and procedures must be revised with a view to obtaining increased efficiency from the individual. Equipment should be simple of operation and maintenance, and, where practicable, should incorporate mechanical devices for eliminating the human factor.

24. Insofar as practicable, all equipment and supplies should be designed and packaged so they can be transported by man, animal, plane, glider or ship.

25. Development of air transport and Army Ground Forces equipment should be coordinated, with the objective that all equipment of standard divisions may be transported by air.

26. Where two or more Technical Services are to participate in development of an item of equipment, responsibility for attaining timely coordination and collateral planning of design should rest on the Service having responsibility for the development of the basic item.

27. Where practicable, the Army and Navy should use the same caliber weapons and interchangeable ammunition.

It is recommended that:

1. The measures necessary to assure the continuous availability of an adequate supply of atomic bombs, and suitable carriers thereof, be accorded priority over all other National Defense projects.

2. The Chemical Warfare Service be assigned a specific mission for developing biological and chemical agents for offensive warfare and be charged with the responsibility of devising defensive measures against such agents, to include the protection of the civil population.

3. Concepts of warfare and locations of strategic outlying bases be reviewed continuously in accordance with anticipated developments in weapons and other agents of warfare.

4. Military Intelligence be assigned the mission of obtaining from all possible sources, including use of its own personnel, information of the intentions, scientific programs, industrial trends and war potentials of foreign countries; and be charged with the ultimate responsibility for presenting timely and accurate information to the Chief of Staff of the Army.

5. War Department Planning Agencies be directed to take measures to assure widest dissemination to the public of information about modern weapons and their effect on an industrial nation.

6. A Directorate of Research and Development be established as an additional General Staff Division on the Directorate level of the War Department, to supersede the New Developments Division of the Special Staff, with personnel and mission as indicated in paragraph 12 a, Section I, Part A.

7. Scientific talent within the Army be encouraged and continuity be assured as indicated in paragraph 12 b, Section I, Part A.

8. This report be adopted as the initial basic guide for equipping the postwar Army. The principal items of equipment and general military characteristics thereof will be found in Part B.

9. A force of combined Arms, under specially selected alert and progressive commanders, be designated to conduct extended service tests of new weapons and equipment, and to formulate tactical doctrine for its employment.

10. Procurement procedure be tested periodically by the awarding of contracts, production and issuance of equipment to the testing force of combined Arms under simulated conditions of urgency.

11. A War Department Equipment Board, consisting of senior commanders from the field commands, be convened periodically to review the progress made in equipment and to modify or revise the basic guide for equipping the Army.

12. A striking force of combined Arms be organized, equipped with the most modern weapons, and trained in all phases of land, airborne and amphibious operations, with the objective that it be instantly available to meet any military contingency.

13. Airborne training be made of Army-wide application.

14. Cavalry be discontinued as a separate Arm.

15. Training data and procedures be studied and revised to raise the efficiency of the individual to a point more nearly commensurate with the inherent efficiency of his weapons and equipment.

16. Continued close cooperation between Army Ground Forces and Army Air Forces in the development of all phases of airborne operations.

PART B

SECTION I

GENERAL TREND OF DEVELOPMENT

1. <u>Atomic Bomb</u>. a. Other than as an explosive, there is no application of nuclear energy anticipated within the predictable future. The explosive is not adaptable for use in artillery weapons. The radioactive materials present in the production of atomic explosive may become agents of warfare. The principal use of the atomic bomb would appear to be against remunerative targets such as cities, vital industrial areas, ports, naval concentrations and bases. Against dispersed troops in the open, its effect would be minimized. Although definite data are not available, it appears likely that its value is lessened by subterranean protection. The explosive may be carried by an aircraft as a bomb or, upon perfection of rockets and guided missiles, may be used in a warhead. Possession of the atomic bomb by a potential enemy renders acute the danger of a sneak attack without declaration of war. Given a sufficient number of bombs, a minimum number of carrier vehicles could accomplish maximum damage. It is conceivable that the damage to our industries could be so extensive as to require the Army to fight a large part of the war with equipment then on hand. Countermeasures must include provision for dispersion and interception of the bomb <u>carrier</u> before it reaches the target, protection against radioactive aftermath, and immediate and devastating retaliation.

b. The only defense apparent at present against a surprise attack with atomic bombs or rockets is dispersion and shelter underground. Industry in this country cannot be expected to disperse to the extent necessary, or go to the expense of building underground plants. The best defense appears to be to convince the entire population of potential enemy countries that this country is prepared to retaliate immediately on any aggressor, and will answer any unprovoked attack by wholesale devastation produced by atomic bombs, biological agents and lethal gases of great intensity.

2. <u>Biological and Chemical Warfare</u>. Biological agents are of such astounding toxicity that their use in warfare might easily result in victory for the user. New lethal chemical agents, a thousandfold more toxic, must be anticipated. Offensively, the problem is one of method of distribution. Defensively, methods of detection and protective devices must be perfected, including those for the civil population. The Chemical Warfare Service should be given specific responsibility for the development of the necessary countermeasures.

3. <u>Airborne Operations</u>. It is probable that the next war will open with a quick surprise attack, followed by retaliation with bombing, long range missiles and biological agents. Regardless of the damage that can be accomplished by retaliatory means, it is probable that a decision can be reached only by occupation of the hostile territory. To sieze and hold advance bases

and other vital points, airborne units will be necessary. All equipment of standard divisions should be capable of being airborne, and consideration should be given to Army-wide airborne training. All facilities for airborne training should be continued in operation and all units should be qualified for airborne use.

4. Aircraft. Planes may be armored, will fly at supersonic speeds at great altitudes, and will be able to bomb accurately under all conditions of weather. The present trend to rocket and jet propelled aircraft affords increased speed at high altitudes. The increased speed, particularly as supersonic speed is approached, may adversely affect efficient operation against ground targets. Without retarding development of strategic aircraft, certain types should be earmarked for development along lines more commensurate with the role of tactical aircraft in support of ground operations.

5. Guided Missiles. Guided missiles, winged or non-winged, traveling at extreme altitudes and at velocities in excess of supersonic speed, are inevitable. Intercontinental ranges of over 3,000 miles and pay load sufficient to carry atomic explosive are to be expected. Remotely controlled, and equipped with homing devices designed to be attracted to sound, metal or heat, such missiles would be incapable of interception with any existing equipment such as fighter aircraft and antiaircraft fire. Guided interceptor missiles, dispatched in accordance with electronically computed data obtained from radar detection stations, will be required. The use of such missiles may be used as an argument for neglecting ground combat equipment. The reverse is true. The necessity for immediately available ground forces is emphasized. An analysis of the use of German V-2 missiles reveals that the only successful countermeasure was the capture of the launching sites by ground forces. Future launching sites may be at sea, in the air, or on the ground.

6. Rockets. Rockets of light artillery caliber for use on the battlefield are an accomplished fact. Larger calibers of much greater range are probable within the predictable future. Fired from a tube, the rocket affords the lightest weapon for saturation of an area with explosives. The drawback is lack of accuracy for point target fire. Such accuracy, if obtained, will come only after a long period of research and development. Therefore, for the foreseeable future, conventional artillery will remain the principal supporting weapon on the battlefield, with the rocket in a supplementary role. It appears that the rocket may be capable of supplementing conventional artillery in the field of super-heavy weapons. However, development data and experience with some very heavy artillery weapons should be obtained in case of failure of the larger caliber rockets to prove themselves as battlefield weapons.

7. Conventional Artillery. Existing artillery weapons appear to have been developed to such a degree that a material increase in efficiency cannot

be expected until basic research is successful in developing new principles of design. The same appears to be true with existing types of propellants. Present ammunition can be further developed profitably. In
particular, research into the merits of a fin-stabilized projectile indicates that greater accuracy and range can be obtained. Gun design might
be materially affected by employment of smooth-bore tubes.

8. Recoilless Weapons. The recoilless weapon is efficient as a portable direct fire gun for Infantry. It is not apparent that the recoilless
weapon will supplant conventional artillery. Recoilless weapons should be
developed in artillery calibers for special purposes. Research should be
conducted into the feasibility of combining the recoilless principle with
conventional recoil mechanisms to reduce the overall gun weight of artillery.

9. Antiaircraft Artillery. Increased speed and higher altitudes of
aircraft pose a problem to the development of antiaircraft weapons. In
general, the trend of development should be to super-velocity, high cyclic
rate, automatic weapons. Long range weapons must be effective at altitudes
up to at least 60,000 feet. Development of radar type equipment to detect
the approach of hostile aircraft, compute fire control data, and apply the
data to the gun, is of prime importance. Inherent limitations of relatively short range and long time of flight exist in all conventional artillery.
Even with developments now foreseen, it is unlikely that antiaircraft artillery will be effective against missiles traveling at speeds in excess of
1,000 miles per hour and at very high altitudes. Guided interceptor missiles will be required to augment the conventional guns.

10. Seacoast Artillery. Fixed seacoast weapons are essential for the
protection of distant or island bases, but less essential under continental
conditions where long coast lines afford many landing opportunities. Therefore, modernization of fixed defenses should proceed with first priority to
the Panama Canal and other outlying bases.

11. Armor. The continuous race between thickness of protective armor
and effectiveness of tank guns would lead progressively to larger and more
cumbersome tanks if uncontrolled. In future development, any conflicting
requirements between mobility and gun power as opposed to protective armor
should be resolved in favor of mobility and gun power. The best antitank
weapon is a better tank. The thin-skinned, self-propelled tank destroyer
has too limited a role to warrant further development now that comparable gun
power can be attained in tank development. Similarly, the towed tank destroyer is outmoded. The armor program should include a light tank for reconnaissance and security missions; a medium tank for exploitation; and a heavy tank
of such gun power that it can destroy any weapon the enemy may place on the
battlefield. Personnel carriers should be full-track, with overhead armor
for protection against airbursts. Two sizes, 12-man and 26-man, will meet
the needs of all Arms for personnel, cargo, or weapons carriers, and for
protected vehicles for forward command posts and vital communications centers.

12. <u>Infantry</u>. No device has been developed to replace the Infantryman on the battlefield; each new development in warfare makes the task of
the Infantryman more important, more difficult and more hazardous. This
is an ominous future for the Arm that in the past war suffered 75% of all
Ground Force casualties. Serious study must be given to all means for
prolonging the battle life of the infantry soldier. The development of
body armor should be given high priority. The movement of Infantry in
armored carriers as far forward as possible should become routine. Investigation should be made of the possibility of extending mechanization to
the extent of a one-man carrier, where the soldier is transported lying down.

13. <u>Cavalry</u>. No further need can be seen for Cavalry as a separate
Arm. However, equipment for both mechanized and horse units is included
herein in the event Cavalry is to be retained in the postwar Army. Whether
performed by Cavalry or by organic reconnaissance units, vehicular ground
reconnaissance will remain a requirement, and such units should utilize the
equipment prescribed for mechanized Cavalry. The armored car lacks the mobility necessary for use by the most advanced patrol elements and the firepower for immediate close support of those elements. Development should be
terminated. The supporting backbone of reconnaissance units should be the
light tank. A lightly armored $\frac{1}{4}$-ton type vehicle should be provided for
use by the most advanced patrol elements.

14. <u>Engineer</u>. Two outstanding problems require solution. There is no
satisfactory mine detector or mine removal equipment, and research on this
equipment must be given high priority. The construction of roads, approaches,
and landing strips requires a tremendous outlay of manpower and ever larger
construction equipment. New methods must be sought, such as the use of soil
stabilization agents, so that roads and landing strips can be constructed
more rapidly. Commercial practice cannot be relied upon entirely to give us
what is needed; the impetus must come from the Corps of Engineers itself.

15. <u>Medical</u>. The value of air transport for the habitual evacuation of
casualties from the army rear area has been demonstrated beyond question.
The system should be extended by placing in forward areas light helicopter
aircraft ambulances for the evacuation of wounded. The objective should be
the evacuation of the casualty from the battlefield to a bed in the permanent
place of treatment in the minimum of time and with the minimum number of intermediate stops. Division and army medical units and channels of evacuation should be reorganized and equipped to accomplish that objective.

16. <u>Ammunition</u>. The outstanding needs are for smokeless and flashless
powder; increased velocity, particularly for tank and antiaircraft use;
simplification of types of fuzes; and uniformity in manufacture so that no
firing data corrections are required for different lots of ammunition. The
VT type fuze affords air bursts that reach the open foxhole and open top
armored carriers and necessitates constant overhead cover for stationary individuals and installations of front line units. The fuze is not capable of

mass production commensurate with the quantities required and it can be jammed by hostile electronic devices. Mass production methods should be perfected and the fuzes made and packaged in assorted wave lengths to reduce the probability of jamming.

17. Communications. At present a commander of Infantry cannot communicate by radio with a supporting tank battalion, air squadron, or similar unit, unless one or the other exchanges an organic radio set. The outstanding need is for an integrated communications system wherein any component of a fighting team may communicate by organic means with any other component of the team. The system should enable the linking together of wire and voice radio channels, with speech security devices incorporated therein, so that the user may be unconcerned as to whether wire, radio, or a combination of both is being used for his conversation.

18. Radar. Radar will serve a multiplicity of needs in fire direction and control, detection of targets, and control of missiles in flight. In its present stage of development it has two inherent limitations; it can be jammed by hostile interference, and its range is limited to a line of sight bounded by the horizon, whether natural or artificial. There is good prospect that the jamming may be overcome. No method is presently known for overcoming the limitation of line of sight, except by temporary expedients of elevating the device, by balloon or otherwise, to lengthen the range to the horizon. This is of outstanding importance, as lack of range may require re-evaluation and relocation of strategic outlying bases, and the provision of additional bases for the establishment of a net of detection stations for the interception of hostile guided missiles and aircraft bearing atomic explosive.

19. Transportation. Motor vehicles should have maximum interchangeability of parts, ease of maintenance and light weight. As one means of accomplishing these ends, competitive bidding should be eliminated. A series of standard chassis groups should be established with parts completely interchangeable within each group. The use of light alloys should be included in future specifications. Imaginative design should be encouraged to obtain increased power, traction and floatation of all vehicles.

SECTION II

INFANTRY EQUIPMENT

General

1. World War II showed conclusively that the task of the Infantryman is the most difficult in modern war. It is imperative, therefore, that the Infantryman be provided with the best equipment that this nation can produce. Improvements in infantry equipment should stress:

    a. Reduction in weight. The highest priority in the allocation of lightweight materials must be accorded manborne and man-handled equipment.

    b. Simplicity of operation. Men cannot be relied upon to perform complex mechanical operations under the stress of battle.

    c. Provision for man-packing. Insofar as practicable all infantry weapons and equipment should be capable of being separated into component loads, weighing not more than 25 pounds.

Individual Arms

2. Individual infantry weapons must possess the greatest possible fire power, lightness and ruggedness.

3. Pistols and Revolvers. a. The pistol should be retained as an infantry weapon. However, a lighter weight pistol, improved to enable the user to obtain greater accuracy, should be developed.

    b. There is no requirement for a revolver in the military service.

4. Rifle, Caliber .30. a. The present caliber .30 rifle, M1, is too heavy for a personal weapon. It should be replaced by a new lightweight caliber .30 rifle of the following general military characteristics: seven pounds maximum weight; capable of selective semiautomatic and automatic fire, with rate of fire approximately 700 rounds per minute; and ballistic performance approximately equivalent to that of the present standard rifle. It should be equipped with a bayonet, grenade launcher, and flash hider. Such changes in the design of the ammunition as are necessary in the production of the new lightweight rifle should be made.

    b. There are presently under development two methods of converting the rifle, M1, to provide both semiautomatic and automatic fire. Pending development and procurement of the new lightweight rifle, a number of rifles, M1, sufficient to equip and train all infantry riflemen in units of the postwar Army, should be converted to provide both semiautomatic and automatic fire by utilization of the most feasible conversion method under development.

5. <u>Carbines and Submachine Guns</u>. The present caliber .30 carbine, M2, should be retained. There is no further requirement for a submachine gun.

6. <u>Grenades</u>. A more efficient hand grenade utilizing an impact fuze, capable of both offensive and defensive use, and weighing approximately 14 ounces, should be developed. A more efficient rifle grenade is required. See Section XVI, Ammunition.

7. <u>Rifle, Caliber .22</u>. As the present caliber .22 rifle was designed to train men in the operation of the caliber .30 rifle, M1903, a new caliber .22 rifle is required for use in training men in the operation of the new lightweight caliber .30 rifle proposed in paragraph 4 above.

Organizational Weapons

8. <u>Machine Gun, Caliber .30</u>. A new, all purpose, caliber .30 machine gun should be developed which, when adopted, would replace the Browning Automatic Rifle when fired from a bipod, and would replace all present caliber .30 machine guns when fired from a tripod. The proposed all purpose, caliber .30 machine gun should possess the following military characteristics: twenty pounds maximum weight; 1800 yards maximum effective range; automatic fire with selective cyclic rates of 1200 and 600 rounds per minute; quick change barrel; disintegrating belt feed; and flash hider. Bipod and tripod mounts should be of the lightest practicable weight.

9. <u>Machine Gun, Caliber .50</u>. a. There is no further requirement for the caliber .50 water-cooled machine gun.

b. The caliber .50 air-cooled machine gun should be retained. The weight of the gun and its ground mount should be reduced.

10. <u>Rocket Launchers</u>. The bazooka type rocket is invaluable for employment against tanks, bunkers, pill boxes and caves. Both the 2.36-inch and 3.5-inch launchers should be retained. Development of launchers and rockets should be continued to provide a night sight; further reduction of the back flash from both the muzzle and the breech; and increased range, accuracy and armor penetration.

11. <u>Mortars</u>. a. The standard 60mm mortar furnishes either bipod fire or one man operation with the tube hand-held. This mortar should be retained.

b. The present 81mm mortar employs a two-piece barrel and a two-piece base plate, which enables it to be used either as a short or long barrel weapon. This mortar should be retained. An additional type of ammunition, weighing approximately fifteen pounds and providing approximately 2000 yards maximum range, should be developed.

c. There is a need for some simple means of lobbing both 60mm and 81mm mortar shells onto reverse slopes at ranges as short as 100 to 200

yards. Such means should be developed.

d. The 4.2-inch chemical mortar proved very effective in close support of Infantry. The 105mm mortar was under development at the conclusion of the war, and pilot models had been tested. Only one mortar of this general caliber is required in the Infantry. Therefore, a mortar should be developed which combines the best features of the 4.2-inch chemical mortar and the 105mm mortar.

e. The success of the recoilless principle warrants thorough examination of the practicability of its application to all mortars. Recoilless reaction chambers should be developed for all infantry mortars, with a view to their use either as high angle or flat trajectory weapons.

12. Infantry Antitank Gun. a. The 57mm gun has become outmoded as an infantry antitank and direct fire weapon. It should be eliminated, as recoilless weapons are more efficient for those missions.

b. In addition to recoilless weapons, which fulfill only part of the requirement for antitank defense, there is a need for a self-propelled, high-velocity, armored antitank gun in the Infantry. See Section VIII, Armored and Tank Destroyer Equipment.

13. Infantry Cannon. The infantry cannon company must be equipped with a self-propelled, armored cannon in order to fulfill its mission. The towed 105mm howitzer, M3, lacks battlefield mobility and protection and should be replaced by a tank mounting a 105mm howitzer.

14. Tanks. There is a requirement for organic tanks within the infantry division, to provide close support for the foot troops throughout the assault.

15. Recoilless Guns. Recoilless guns are valuable infantry weapons and the 57mm, 75mm, and 105mm recoilless guns should be further developed. See Section XV, Recoilless Guns.

16. Flame Throwers. The use of flame, particularly in cave warfare, has exceeded all expectations. There is a need for a portable flame thrower of the most efficient design. See Section XII, Chemical Warfare Equipment.

Special Vehicles

17. Armored Vehicles. The ever increasing effectiveness of field artillery fire and the advent of the VT fuze make it necessary to provide maximum protection for troops and vital installations functioning in forward areas. A completely armored full track vehicle to serve as a communication center, and a completely armored full track personnel carrier should be developed. See Section VIII, Armored and Tank Destroyer Equipment.

18. Weasel Type Carrier. The weasel type carrier has proved to be

efficient for operation over difficult terrain and further development should be continued. See Section XX, Transportation Equipment.

Organizational Equipment

19. **Radar and Sound Detection Equipment.** a. A requirement exists in the infantry for a means of determining troop movements under conditions of poor visibility; for detecting targets; for controlling the fire of weapons; and for locating concealed enemy weapons. Some progress has been made in the development of a radar mortar locator and the sound locator. Development of that equipment should be continued. See Section XIX, Radar Equipment.

b. **Outpost Audio Detector Set.** There is a requirement for a lightweight audio amplifier detector set which will enable front line troops, during conditions of poor visibility, to detect approaching hostile ground troops at distances beyond the range of hearing. A detector set, weighing approximately seven pounds and composed of two or more microphones connected by short leads to an audio amplifier and headset, should be developed.

20. **Infra-Red Equipment.** a. The trend to night operations indicates a need for development of aids thereto. The success of night viewing devices employing infra-red principles dictates increased military exploitation of the infra-red field. Development of infra-red equipment should include increased range of devices for detection of enemy targets; battlefield illumination; night operation of vehicles without visible lights; and beacons and homing devices. See Section VII, Engineer Equipment.

b. There should be developed a means which will permit writing or reading at night without the use of visible light.

21. **Mine Detectors.** No thoroughly satisfactory method of detecting mines and mine fields has as yet been devised. A light, highly sensitive, universal type mine detector should be developed. See Section VII, Engineer Equipment.

22. **Communication Equipment.** a. Further improvement in communications equipment should provide:

(1) Better field wire; improved power reels; and suitable radio relay.

(2) A lightweight teletypewriter capable of working on both wire and radio circuits.

(3) Smaller, lighter, and more portable switchboards and multi-channel radio telephone communication.

(4) An integrated infantry-tank-artillery-air voice radio,

and a portable radio to provide communications be-
tween dismounted men and individual tanks.

    (5) An electronic device which will turn speech into
printed words at the receiving station.

    b. For a detailed discussion of communications equipment, see Sec-
tion XVII, Communication Equipment.

    23. <u>Protective Equipment</u>. Casualties suffered by the infantry soldier
in this war represent 75% of the casualties suffered by the entire Ground
Forces. It is of the utmost importance that development of protective clothing and equipment keep abreast of the increased casualty effect of the various weapons of warfare.

    a. Lighter, flexible body armor for protection against small arms
fire and shell fragments should be provided.

    b. The helmet should be improved to provide minimum weight while
retaining the protection and coverage of the present helmet.

    c. Anti-mine shoes, which can be worn over regular footgear, de-
crease ground pressure thereby permitting an individual to safely negotiate
emplaced mine fields. They should be further developed.

    d. The increased use of fire as a weapon in modern warfare, and
the danger to occupants of closed vehicles from incendiary projectiles, have
created widespread requirement for flameproof clothing. Development should
investigate fabrics which are inherently non-inflammable, as well as means
of flameproofing inflammable fabrics.

    e. The gas mask should be made lighter, with increased canister
efficiency and a more flexible face piece.

    f. There is need for an impregnation treatment of clothing which
is durable, does not materially increase the weight of the clothing, and does
not injuriously affect or irritate the wearer. The need for the development
of clothing which will protect the wearer against radio-active poisons or
radiations produced as by-products of atomic energy warfare should be studied.

    24. <u>Pocket-Size Range Finder</u>. A pocket-size range finder should be de-
veloped.

    25. <u>Lightweight Power Generator</u>. There should be developed a small,
silent, lightweight, all purpose power generator to furnish electrical energy
for front line command posts.

SECTION III

CAVALRY EQUIPMENT

General

1. The Board considered equipment for both Horse and Mechanized Cavalry so that both categories would be provided for if they should be continued in the postwar Army. If, as recommended by the Board, the Cavalry is abolished, all references in this section to Mechanized Cavalry apply with equal force to reconnaissance elements used by the Armored Force, and all references to Horse Cavalry equipment should be deleted.

2. Combat experience in the recent war has demonstrated that Mechanized Cavalry Reconnaissance Units, in addition to their prescribed role of reconnaissance, will be called upon frequently to perform offensive and defensive combat. Equipment considered herein provides for such contingencies.

Individual Weapons

3. Cavalry personnel of both Horse and Mechanized units require individual weapons incorporating the features set forth in Section II, Infantry Equipment.

Organizational Weapons

4. a. The cavalry's requirements for organizational weapons can be met satisfactorily by selection from the types recommended in Section II, Infantry Equipment; and in Section IV, Field Artillery Equipment.

    b. The existing 75mm pack howitzer should be further developed to reduce overall weight through utilization of lighter metals.

Organizational Equipment

5. <u>Combat Vehicles.</u> a. Requirements exist in the Mechanized Cavalry for the following types:

    (1) Lightly armored $\frac{1}{4}$-ton truck.

    (2) Light tank.

    (3) Armored assault gun, 105mm howitzer.

    (4) Full-track armored personnel carrier, mortar carrier and command vehicle.

    b. (1) In addition to its current mission, the present light tank, M 24, should replace the armored car, and further development of the light tank should provide silent overall operation, silent tracks and extended cruising range.

        (2) To extend the effectiveness of motor reconnaissance and to

carry out any missions formerly performed by the armored car that cannot be performed effectively by the light tank, there should be developed a lightly armored ¼-ton truck.

    (3) The requirement for the armored assault gun should be met initially by utilization of the current M37 type, and later by an improved type with overhead splinterproof armor as indicated in Section IV, Field Artillery Equipment.

    c. The general characteristics of the lightly armored ¼-ton truck, light tank, and full track armored carriers are contained in Section VIII, Armored and Tank Destroyer Equipment.

    6. <u>Remote Control Device</u>. Research and development should be initiated to produce a remote control device for vehicular installation by means of which a crewless vehicle could be directed in advance of the controlling vehicle to draw hostile fire, to aid in disclosing or locating enemy weapons, or to disclose enemy mines and road blocks.

    7. <u>Motor Vehicles</u>. Motor vehicles which are currently in use, or recommended for development in Section XX, Transportation Equipment, will meet the requirements of Cavalry.

    8. <u>Horse Equipment</u>. a. Present standard Saddles, Phillips, Pack, Cargo, and those now being standardized, are satisfactory and adequately fill the requirement for use at varying gaits and animal weights.

    b. Simultaneously with the adoption of any new equipment for Horse Cavalry, development should be initiated to provide suitable hangers and related equipment for transport by cargo saddles.

    c. Advances made in metallurgy, fabrics, plastics, and other appropriate synthetic materials should be utilized in animal equipment where suitable, to decrease weight, increase durability, and increase moisture repellency.

    9. <u>Communication Equipment</u>. a. The general requirements of Cavalry for improved communication equipment are similar to those of other Arms, as set forth in Section XVII, Communication Equipment.

    b. Communication problems in the Cavalry, complicated by frequent tactical disposition over extensive fronts and distances from forward to rear elements, require an integrated system of radios which will permit communication within the various elements of Cavalry and with the echelons of command of other Arms with which Cavalry units usually operate. The equipment should incorporate selective dial type of communication, with security or speech scrambling devices integral in the equipment.

    c. There is a requirement for television transmitting and receiving equipment capable of installation and transport in light tanks and light reconnaissance airplanes.

d. Page style facsimile equipment, equal at least in size to the standard message blank, is required for radio transmission of orders, small maps, and sketches. The equipment should be capable of installation in appropriate tactical vehicles.

e. Equipment for communication by modulated light beam is required as a supplementary means of close-in communication.

10. <u>Radar Equipment</u>. There is a requirement for the following, the details of which are covered in Section XIX, Radar Equipment:

a. Equipment, for use by patrols, observation groups, and individuals, which will give warning of the location or movement, under all conditions, of enemy personnel, vehicles, and installations. Suitable types should be developed for use by dismounted personnel and for vehicular mounting.

b. Means for fire control and for guiding the movement of individuals.

c. A homing device which will enable continuous orientation of individuals.

Miscellaneous

11. <u>Odograph</u>. There should be developed a simpler, more accurate, non-magnetic odograph for mounting in vehicles and a similar device capable of being carried by a dismounted individual.

12. <u>Range Finder</u>. A compact range finder should be developed for use by dismounted individuals.

13. <u>Anti-Chemical Protection for Animals</u>. Development should be continued to provide simple, effective equipment to protect animals against vapor and liquid chemicals. Items should be limited to improved protective mask and goggles, and protective ointment.

14. <u>Animal Rations</u>. Research and experiment should be continued to develop suitable compact forage, both grain and grassy types, which will provide sufficient nutrition and bulk and simplify the supply of animals in the field.

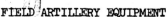

SECTION IV

FIELD ARTILLERY EQUIPMENT

General

1. In future military operations, as in the past, Field Artillery will be the principal supporting arm to Infantry and Armor in their role of seizing and holding ground. This mission requires both high angle and flat trajectory weapons of towed and self-propelled types.

2. Present field artillery weapons are of the desired calibers and types necessary for the accomplishment of all missions, except that of very large caliber weapons for destruction and for large area coverage. The latter mission appears to be appropriate for rockets, guided missiles, and all-weather air bombing. However, since the development of rockets, guided missiles, and improved air bombing may fail to meet the need for these large caliber missions on both area and point targets, and the need for assured close support in all weather, the present development of certain large caliber weapons for field artillery purposes to fill the requirement for these fire missions should be continued.

3. a. In general, existing field artillery weapons have reached a stage of development where, under current technology, major redesign of a weapon would obtain only a relatively small increase in efficiency. Only after research has revealed new means, such as greatly improved metals, will major changes in design be profitable. However, ammunition can be improved, without major changes in the design of weapons, to secure greater accuracy and effectiveness of fire.

b. First priority with respect to improving the efficiency of existing field artillery weapons should be accorded to projects pertaining to increase in accuracy and improvement of ammunition, and to the improvement of devices for the finding of targets and the control of fire. Second priority should be accorded to projects for the improvement of carriages and tubes.

4. Recent ballistic investigations indicate the feasibility of developing fin-stabilized projectiles of considerably improved ballistic efficiency for launching from smooth bore cannon. If successful, such development may result in the progressive displacement of present conventional artillery types.

Weapons

5. The trend of development is toward both self-propelled and towed mounts for all field artillery weapons except the very light and the very heavy special purpose types. In principle, the same weapon should be used on both self-propelled and towed mounts. Since the self-propelled mount presents the greater difficulties in development, the weapon should be designed, as a general rule, for the self-propelled mount and adapted to the towed mount.

6. a. No special weapons for special operations, such as for jungle, arctic, desert, mountain, airborne and amphibious types of warfare, are listed herein. Experience indicates that present weapons, with those under development, afford sufficient types suitable or adaptable for these purposes.

b. Artillery weapons in armored divisions should be of the self-propelled type and be provided with splinter-proof armor, including overhead protection against airburst.

7. The following existing types of weapons are necessary for the Field Artillery to accomplish its missions and should be retained:

Guns		Howitzers		Mortars	
Caliber	Range (yds)	Caliber	Range (yds)	Caliber	Range (yds)
		Towed Types			
		75mm(pack)	9,600		
		105mm	12,500	*105mm or	
155mm	25,700	155mm	16,000	4.2-inch	6,500
8-inch	35,000	8-inch	18,500		
		240mm	25,000		
		Self-Propelled Types			
		105mm	12,500		
155mm	25,700	155mm	16,000		
		8-inch	18,500		

*Also discussed in Section II, Infantry Equipment, for infantry use.

8. Development of the following weapons, now in process, should be continued:

Guns		Howitzers		Mortars	
					(yds at
Caliber	Range (yds)	Caliber	Range (yds)	Caliber	Range least)
		Towed Types			
**105mm	25,000	None	******	155mm	10,000
				8-10-inch	10,000
				36-inch	10,000
		Self-Propelled Types			
**105mm	25,000	240mm	25,200	155mm	10,000
8-inch	35,000			8-10-inch	10,000

**Either the high velocity tank gun or antiaircraft gun, both of which are at present under development, should be selected to fill this need.

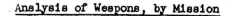

Analysis of Weapons, by Mission

9. a. <u>Close Support</u>. The infantry must be able to follow artillery fire close enough to permit them to rush hostile positions before the enemy has time to react after artillery fire is lifted. The present 105mm howitzer satisfies this requirement within reasonable limits.

b. <u>Support at Medium Ranges</u>. To deepen and add weight to fire of the 105mm howitzer, the 155mm and 8-inch howitzers and the 155mm gun are necessary.

c. <u>Long Range Fire Support</u>. For long range missions the 8-inch gun and 240mm howitzer are required.

d. <u>Extremely Long Range Fires</u>. It is anticipated that, with expected improvements, rockets, guided missiles, and all-weather air bombing should meet this requirement. In the event that such expectations are not realized, larger caliber, long range howitzers and guns, not included in this report, may be required.

e. <u>Large Volume Surprise, Area, Interdiction, and Harassing Fires</u>. Present standard weapons are necessary for these fires. These weapons may be materially augmented by rockets, guided missiles and mortars.

Motor Vehicles

10. General transport requirements for field artillery are outlined in Section XX, Transportation Equipment. The following special purpose vehicles are required:

a. A mobile, armored observation post tender which will enable personnel to cross fire-swept zones. See Section VIII, Armored and Tank Destroyer Equipment.

b. Tractor, high speed, light.

c. Tractor, high speed, medium.

d. Tractor, high speed, heavy.

e. Wrecker, full-track.

f. A lightweight, track-laying reconnaissance vehicle of about 1½-ton capacity, weasel type. See Section XX, Transportation Equipment.

g. An improved cargo trailer suitable for the transport of ammunition.

h. (1) A crane capable of handling maximum field artillery loads. This crane should be mounted on a standard heavy full-track

prime mover.

(2) Bulldozer blades of the folding type for mounting on the front of prime movers and self-propelled carriages.

Miscellaneous

11. Ammunition. Section XVI, Ammunition, covers Field Artillery requirements for projectiles, fuzes, propellants, and ammunition packaging.

12. Communication Equipment. In forward areas, radio is the vital necessity in communication, as the efficiency of artillery support will be dependent upon it. Wire, in forward areas, should be considered a secondary or alternate means of communication. The development of equipment applicable to the Field Artillery is discussed in Section XVII, Communication Equipment.

13. Radar. Development of radar for surveillance, adjustment, fire control, mortar and artillery detection, target finding and locating, determining meteorological data, survey and navigation should be continued. Of special importance is the development of radar or other means for fire control at the longer ranges. See Section XIX, Radar Equipment.

14. Television. The use of television for adjustment of fire, surveillance, reconnaissance, survey and mapping should be developed. See Section XVII, Communication Equipment, and Section XVIII, Survey, Observation and Meteorological Equipment.

15. Survey, Observation and Meteorological Equipment. Requirements for this type of equipment are discussed in Section XVIII, Survey, Observation and Meteorological Equipment.

16. Field Artillery Observation Airplane. The importance of the observation airplane will continue to increase. Improvements in maneuverability, load carrying capacity, length of flight, visibility, take-off and landing speeds are necessary. Radios, photographic equipment and television for this type of plane should continue to be developed. See Section XI, Air Support Equipment.

17. Deceptive Equipment. There are requirements for flash and sound simulators, lighter weight camouflage, and devices to prevent the location of artillery by hostile radar.

SECTION V

SEACOAST ARTILLERY EQUIPMENT

General

1. Combat experiences in the recent war indicate that seacoast fortifications must be capable of all-around resistance to land, air and sea attack.

2. The casemate type of seacoast artillery emplacement provides inadequate protection, too low a rate of fire, and a too restricted field of fire; and, therefore, is obsolescent. The naval turret meets the requirement for modern fixed seacoast artillery, and the policy should be one of utilization of the most modern Navy turrets and weapons, modified for installation on land.

3. In the development of new equipment for seacoast fortifications, timely provisions should be made to permit the Corps of Engineers to initiate the collateral planning necessary for installation of this equipment. Continuous study should be directed toward a determination of the requirements for protection of emplacements against attack by air, heavy artillery, land or naval, and chemicals.

4. Guided Missiles. Guided missiles appear to have a definite place in future seacoast defenses. Future development of guided missiles may render obsolete the larger calibers of seacoast artillery. Development should encompass both aerial and waterborne guided missiles. Maximum range consistent with accuracy and destructive effect against armored ships should be provided. See Section XIV, Guided Missiles.

Weapons

5. Fixed Seacoast Artillery. Fixed seacoast artillery for the protection of vital areas must be of the turret type in order to achieve all-around fields of fire, gain higher rates of fire, and secure adequate protection for personnel and equipment. Modern naval turrets modified by increasing the top, side, and back armor are readily adaptable for fixed land installations. The following naval turrets and weapons should be adopted for fixed seacoast artillery:

    a. 5-inch dual-purpose.

    b. 6-inch dual-purpose.

    c. 8-inch single-purpose.

    d. 16-inch single-purpose.

6. Mobile Seacoast Artillery. Mobile seacoast artillery is required

for temporary installations and the reinforcement of fixed seacoast defenses. Standard artillery and antiaircraft artillery weapons, with necessary modifications and auxiliary equipment, should be utilized to fill these requirements. The 155mm Gun, M1, mounted on Firing Platform, M1, with Data Transmission System, T-21, meets the current need for mobile seacoast artillery.

7. Railway Artillery. Air power has destroyed the effective mobility of railway artillery. Development of this class of weapons should be terminated.

Fire Control Equipment

8. Present designs and types of fire control equipment are generally satisfactory, but development should continue to improve this equipment. Conventional plotting room equipment should be restudied with the view to eliminating unnecessary types and improving overall efficiency.

9. Radars and Computers. Fire control radar and computer elements should be combined into one system. Dual purpose fire control radar-computer combinations should be provided for dual purpose seacoast batteries. On-carriage fire control radar-computer combinations should be considered for turrets.

  a. Computers. Development of computing elements of radar-computers should provide for:

  (1) Reduction in overall weight and size and a reduction in the number of operators required.

  (2) Improved performance to provide prediction for maneuvering courses, automatic computation of fire adjustment corrections and automatic application of ballistic corrections.

  (3) Inclusion of time-of-flight indicators.

  (4) Application of spotting corrections received from remote radar stations.

  b. Mechanical Computers. Simple mechanical gun data computers should be provided for emergency fire control in lieu of present plotting boards.

  c. Radars. There is a requirement for improved fire control radars and surveillance radars in seacoast artillery installations. Research and development should provide the following type sets:

  (1) An ultra-long range surface surveillance radar (250 - 300 miles.)

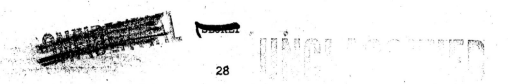

(2) An improved, lightweight surface surveillance radar.

(3) A radar set which is capable of locating a gun or launching platform, though defiladed, by observing a projectile or missile in flight.

(4) A dual purpose fire control radar.

(5) Means of protecting radar antennas from blast and fragments.

d. For desired military characteristics, see Section XIX, Radar Equipment.

Miscellaneous Equipment

10. <u>Ammunition</u>. Ammunition development by the Army and Navy should be coordinated to insure that the ammunition for naval guns and like caliber seacoast artillery weapons are interchangeable, where practicable. There is a requirement for VT and point detonating fuzes for use with high-capacity or high explosive projectiles in all calibers of seacoast artillery. Advantage should be taken of Navy developments along these lines.

11. <u>Mine Equipment</u>. Controlled submarine mines are required to protect vital harbors and anchorages against attack by all types of surface craft and submerged submarines. Present submarine mine equipment must be improved to be effective against all degaussed and sound-proofed submarines and to provide for arsenal loading. Lightweight mine equipment for use in amphibious operations should be developed.

12. <u>Searchlight Equipment</u>. A requirement exists for two types of searchlights; one portable, the other a flood light type for installation in casemates or in turrets. Future development should provide for increased protection and more efficient operation.

13. <u>Parachute Flares</u>. A requirement exists for a multiple or automatic rocket launcher for projecting illuminating parachute flares.

14. <u>Harbor Defense Communications</u>. Present harbor defense communication systems and equipment vary in each harbor defense installation, and in general are outmoded. Modernizing of harbor defenses should include development and installation of a uniform communication system.

SECTION VI

ANTIAIRCRAFT EQUIPMENT

General

1. The trend of developments indicates that antiaircraft targets of the near future will include greatly improved missiles of the V1 and V2 types and partially armored airplanes flying at various speeds up to and including the supersonic and at heights from near the ground to extremely high altitudes. Present antiaircraft equipment cannot cope with such targets. In the past, antiaircraft artillery fulfilled its mission in defense against manned aircraft if the percentage of hostile craft destroyed in each raid was high enough to make the cost to the enemy prohibitive. In future wars, no single airplane or bomb-carrying missile should be permitted to penetrate the defenses of a vital area because of the possibility that it might be carrying an atomic bomb. It is imperative that the effectiveness of antiaircraft equipment be increased until the ultimate obtainable is reached in both conventional and newly conceived types.

2. The solution of the antiaircraft problem should include development of:

a. Conventional type weapons having the greatest obtainable effectiveness.

b. Fire direction and fire control equipment which will be adequate to cope with future targets and obtain the maximum exploitation of the capabilities of the weapons.

c. A guided missile capable of intercepting and destroying aircraft and missiles of the V1 and V2 types. See Section XIV, Guided Missiles.

Conventional Weapons

3. Each type of antiaircraft weapon must have high rate of fire, accuracy, and flexibility; and deliver a projectile of such destructive power and time of flight as to make it effective within its normal range bracket. It should have a secondary role of firing at targets on the ground; however, its effectiveness for antiaircraft purposes should be the paramount consideration in its design. Three types of weapons are necessary; short range, intermediate range, and long range.

4. Short Range Weapons. a. The present .50 caliber machine gun does not have sufficient range or velocity for effective use against targets of the future.

b. An antiaircraft machine gun of suitable caliber should be developed for use at short ranges, from 200 to 2,500 yards, against targets

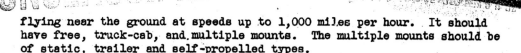

flying near the ground at speeds up to 1,000 miles per hour. It should
have free, truck-cab, and multiple mounts. The multiple mounts should be
of static, trailer and self-propelled types.

5. <u>Intermediate Range Weapons</u>. a. The present standard 37mm and 40mm
automatic cannon have been only partially successful owing to the fact that
a direct hit must be obtained before any damage is inflicted on the target.
The greatly increased target speeds expected in the future necessitate a super-
velocity cannon of caliber large enough to accommodate a VT type fuze.

b. There should be developed an automatic super-velocity cannon
of approximately 75mm caliber, with automatic loading and high cyclic rate,
for use at ranges from 500 to 6,000 yards, against aircraft and V1 type
missiles flying at speeds up to 1,000 miles per hour and at heights up to
15,000 feet. It should have highly mobile trailed and self-propelled mounts
equipped with power controls.

6. <u>Long Range Weapons</u>. a. The present standard long range 90mm and
120mm guns are deficient in muzzle velocity, effective range and the flexibility necessary for use against targets of the future.

b. A mobile, long range antiaircraft gun should be developed for
use at ranges from 2,000 to 27,000 yards, against targets flying at speeds
up to 1,000 miles per hour and at altitudes up to 60,000 feet. The gun
should be of the super-velocity type and should be approximately 105mm caliber, with mechanical loading and power controls. The mount should be a two-
bogie trailed mount possessing the best cross-country mobility obtainable.

c. There is a requirement for a highly mobile type of long range
antiaircraft gun to support divisions in fluid situations. Development of
the long range gun should include a lighter, more mobile model for that purpose. Pending realization of that goal, development of the type T16 experi-
mental 90mm antiaircraft gun should be continued with emphasis on attaining
mobility sufficient to meet the requirement.

Fire Direction and Fire Control

7. At present there is no suitable equipment available to permit the
Antiaircraft Defense Commander of a vital area to properly direct and control the fires of antiaircraft weapons during large scale, concentrated
attacks. There should be developed a completely integrated fire direction
system to provide the following:

a. Independent means for radar surveillance of the entire area
within approximately 200 miles of the defended area, including location
and positive identification of all aerial targets within the area and means
for automatic remote display of this information.

b. Means for continuous and instantaneous transmission and display
of the following data:

(1) Information from Air Force Early Warning and control stations.

(2) Target position data obtained from the foregoing sources, and fire control or direction instructions emanating from the Fire Direction Center to each fire unit in the defense.

(3) Information on all targets being tracked or engaged by all gun elements in the defense suitable for display at the fire direction center or for use in firing by another gun element of the defense.

8. Fire control systems should be developed which, commensurate with restrictions on weight and complexity of equipment, will permit the engagement of any target at maximum range with the greatest accuracy possible. Such equipment should have the following general military characteristics:

a. <u>For Machine Guns</u>. (1) Free and Truck-Cab Type Mounts: A computing sight, mechanical or otherwise, of light, rugged and simple construction, small enough to be mounted on gun without impairing the operation of the gun, and capable of operation by the gunner. The sight should be usable by day or night.

(2) Multiple Mount. A combination on-carriage radar-director capable of locating and tracking seen and unseen targets flying at minimum altitudes and which will permit targets to be engaged effectively at all ranges from 200 to 2,500 yards. An emergency visual tracking system similar to that designed for the free mount also should be provided.

b. <u>For Automatic Cannon</u>. (1) A combination on-carriage radar-director which is capable of radar search and tracking of targets at ranges which will permit bursts to be placed on all seen or unseen targets, at all ranges between 500 and 6,000 yards and at all altitudes up to 15,000 feet. Provisions should be made for both optical and fully automatic tracking. Simultaneous radar search and tracking should be incorporated, if practicable. Director data should be transmitted automatically to the gun.

(2) An on-carriage handlebar controlled computing sight, for emergency fire control.

c. <u>For Guns</u>. A completely integrated battery tactical and fire control unit, capable of engaging all targets at ranges from 2,000 to 27,000 yards, which will provide:

(1) Means for continuous determination of position of all aerial targets within searching range, accurate location of the target being fired upon and the next target to be engaged, with provision for optical tracking when targets are visible, and means of identification when practicable.

(2) Continuous determination of firing data for the two targets being tracked with provision to rapidly switch either set of firing data to the guns.

(3) Means for continuous transmission of present position data to other batteries and fire direction center, and reception of similar data for use in computation of firing data.

(4) Complete battery tactical control to include continuous automatic display of pertinent information and the transmission of necessary commands, signals, identification, etc., with minimum loss of time.

Miscellaneous

9. <u>Antiaircraft Searchlights</u>. Developments in radar have greatly reduced the need for searchlights in the antiaircraft role and may eventually eliminate their use. Therefore, further development of antiaircraft searchlights should be deferred.

10. <u>Barrage Balloons</u>. The automatic weapons recommended herein for development should be capable of delivering accurately directed fire against both seen and unseen targets, in which case, the supplementary use of barrage balloons may become not only useless, but undesirable. No further development of barrage balloon equipment should be undertaken at the present time.

11. <u>Ammunition</u>. Reduction of time of flight and increase in the destructive power of antiaircraft projectiles are of paramount importance and necessitate the most efficient projectiles for use in each type of weapon. The specific developments desired are set forth in Section XVI, Ammunition.

SECTION VII

ENGINEER EQUIPMENT

General

1. Organic engineer equipment should be the same whether the unit is servicing an infantry, cavalry, armored, mountain or airborne division. Engineer equipment comprises three general types: (1) civilian equipment employed without modification for military use, e.g. construction equipment; (2) civilian equipment modified for military use, e.g. reproduction equipment; and (3) equipment developed solely for military use, e.g. bridging equipment.

2. Of outstanding importance is the necessity for developing satisfactory methods and equipment for detection and removal of mines and for rapid road and airstrip construction. These projects should be assigned high priority in the development of engineer equipment.

Construction Equipment

3. In general, civilian construction equipment needs little development by the Army since the goal of rapid, low cost construction in the civilian field will force constant research and development by civilian agencies. Research and liaison with civilian agencies, from the military viewpoint, should be to obtain better mobility under adverse conditions, decreased vulnerability to enemy action with a minimum loss of operating efficiency, and standardization to reduce the spare parts maintenance problem.

4. <u>Soil Stabilizing Agents</u>. In the past, construction of roads and approaches to bridges has required the use of heavier and heavier equipment. There is a need for research and development of new methods for rapid road construction by some means such as soil stabilizing agents.

Mapping and Reproduction Equipment

5. The Army Air Forces should continue to be charged with the responsibility for providing suitable aerial photographs to the Engineers for mapping purposes. The preparation of maps is an Engineer responsibility. Closer coordination of priorities is required to insure that proper photographs are made available to the Engineers when they are needed. This is a function of command.

6. <u>Air Mapping Equipment</u>. In the past, mapping aircraft have been mostly adaptations of existing tactical aircraft. The following types of equipment should be developed by the Army Air Forces specifically to accomplish the engineer mapping mission:

a. A high performance photomapping plane designed solely to obtain suitable mapping photographs at all desired altitudes.

b. A liaison type photographic plane.

c. Aerial mapping cameras suitable for use with the mapping planes, either when equipped with radar surveying equipment or when not so equipped.

d. A fighter type airplane which can be equipped with cameras is required for special purposes.

7. General Equipment. Present mapping and reproduction equipment should be simplified and improved to keep abreast of the latest technological advances. The following types are specifically required:

a. Radar surveying equipment for extending both vertical and horizontal control by aerial means.

b. Rectifying cameras.

c. Process camera.

d. Rapid contact printer.

e. Offset press.

f. Plate processing equipment, including grainer.

g. Gelatin or spirit duplicator.

h. Multiplex equipment.

i. Printing and developing machines for reproduction of tracings.

j. Stereoplotting instruments.

k. Task Force-type reproduction equipment.

8. Special Maps. In addition to the types of maps now produced by the Engineers, equipment and methods should be developed for producing the following:

a. Tank maps for strategic purposes, which will show soil types and consistency under varying meteorological conditions with correlations to indicate tank passability, natural tank obstacles, and terrain impassable to tanks.

b. Improved stereo-pairs and pocket stereoscopes in quantities sufficient for issue down to squad leaders or vehicle commanders.

Water Supply Equipment

9. Present water supply equipment is too heavy and bulky for the amount of water purified and there is no satisfactory equipment for use by patrol

size units. Development of water purification equipment of the following sizes should be continued with a view to reducing weight and increasing efficiency:

    a. A large capacity, portable unit suitable for use with the water supply company.

    b. A medium capacity, portable unit suitable for use with the combat battalion.

    c. A small capacity unit which can be man-packed for use by airborne or mountain divisions.

    d. A squad or patrol size unit.

  10. Equipment should be developed for making salt water potable.

  11. Research should be undertaken to develop a method of water purification in which the objectionable taste of chlorine is eliminated.

Bridging and Stream Crossing Equipment

  12. a. The increase in the weights of vehicles organic in the infantry division and the armored division and projected heavier vehicles and their transporters requires that bridging and stream crossing equipment be developed to meet future needs. There should be an integrated system of bridges with the component parts of all bridges interchangeable, insofar as practicable, without compromising the basic design of any bridge.

    b. All bridging and stream crossing equipment should be capable of erection and use on rivers with high velocity currents with allowance made for rapid changes of water level.

    c. The development of bridge equipment should include development of its transportation and erection equipment.

    d. Except for the foot bridge and the infantry support bridge, which must be capable of erection by manpower alone, it is desirable but not essential that all bridges be capable of erection by manpower alone as an alternate method to the use of powered erection equipment.

    e. Width and type of construction of the roadway of each bridge should be such that it will accommodate all loads and types of treads of vehicles of the unit for which designed. Improvement of bridging should keep pace with the development of vehicles and equipment which must use each bridge.

    f. All bridges should be designed so that they can be erected in the minimum time.

  13. <u>Bridges, Boats and Cableways</u>. The following types of bridging and

stream crossing equipment are required:

    a. <u>Boats</u>.

        (1) An assault boat of high buoyancy, so designed that it can carry an infantry squad and a crew of three or be used in the construction of the infantry support bridge. The boat should have a detachable, silent propulsion unit.

        (2) A storm boat with a silent propulsion unit, capable of carrying an infantry squad and a crew of two across rivers or lakes at high speed.

        (3) A maneuverable reconnaissance boat of six-man capacity with a noiseless propulsion unit.

    b. <u>Bridges</u>.

        (1) A foot bridge which is simple, rugged, readily portable, easily assembled, and invulnerable to small arms fire and shell and bomb fragments.

        (2) An infantry support bridge capable of carrying the ammunition and supply vehicles of the infantry battalion and the light field artillery battalion of the infantry division. It should utilize the assault boat for the floating piers.

        (3) A division floating bridge capable of carrying the bulk of the vehicles which are organic in or normally accompany the infantry or armored division in combat, except for heavy tanks.

        (4) An army floating bridge capable of carrying all loads normally with a field army.

        (5) A super-heavy floating bridge, with two adjacent 11-foot roadways, capable of carrying all military loads.

        (6) A fixed pier bridge for division loads, with one roadway at least 13.5 feet wide, for variable spans up to 150 feet.

        (7) A fixed pier bridge for army loads, with two adjacent 11-foot roadways, for various spans up to 120 feet.

    (8) A fixed pier bridge for super-heavy loads, with two adjacent 11-foot roadways, for variable spans up to 120 feet.

    (9) A fixed pier line of communications bridge for super-heavy loads, with two adjacent 11-foot roadways, for variable spans up to 120 feet. The development of this bridge should be coordinated with the development of a fixed pier railway bridge using the same components to the maximum possible extent.

    (10) A suspension bridge for divisional loads, with a roadway at least 13.5 feet wide, for spans of at least 400 feet.

    (11). Vehicular mounted bridges of the following types for quick launching over relatively narrow gaps primarily to assist the advance of armored units:

        (a) A bridge for assault purposes which will carry light and medium tanks over 40-foot spans and can be placed from the engineer armored combat vehicle.

        (b) A bridge which will carry medium and heavy tanks over 60 to 80-foot spans and can be launched from a lightly armored vehicular carrier.

    c. <u>Cableways</u>. Cableways of the following types for mountain warfare and river crossing operations:

    (1) A supply cableway transportable by pack animals and capable of transporting concentrated loads of supplies and equipment of types required by mountain divisions in forward mountain areas in sufficient volume to supply a combat team over spans up to 1200 feet.

    (2) A lighter man-packed cableway capable of transporting an individual with full field equipment over spans up to 1500 feet.

    (3) A cableway providing all necessary rigging for operation of trail ferries, including DUKWs, LVTs and other amphibious vehicles, for spans up to 1200 feet in rapid river currents.

14. <u>Protective Devices</u>. A requirement exists for bridge protective devices of two types:

    a. A system of booms and nets to protect a bridge against floating mines, swimmers, small submarines, debris, and barges or other craft.

    b. A warning system, of sonic or electronic type (similar to ASDIC), to detect small submarines, swimmers, floating mines and other moving objects, floating or submerged.

Engineer Armored Vehicles

15. The following armored vehicles are required for engineer use:

    a. An armored reconnaissance vehicle.

    b. An armored combat vehicle capable of carrying personnel and cargo and equipped with various attachments such as dozer blade, mine detecting and removing attachments, bridge carrying and laying equipment, and demolition charge launcher.

    c. The above vehicles are discussed in Section VIII, Armored and Tank Destroyer Equipment.

Vehicles

16. The following special purpose vehicles are required:

    a. Because of the greatly increased demands for road and other construction, dump trucks of approximately 4 and 7-ton capacity are needed for use in Corps and Army service areas. The $2\frac{1}{2}$-ton dump truck is suitable for use by combat engineers and should be retained.

    b. A series of cranes and shovels from 3/4-yard to $1\frac{1}{2}$-yard capacity, mounted on standard truck chassis.

    c. An armored tractor for use in forward areas where the operators are exposed to small arms fire and shell fragments.

    d. A tractor with low ground pressure for towing vehicles and supply sleds through areas where the ground is soft.

    e. Dozer blades for mounting on tanks and amphibious tractors, for removing obstacles while under fire.

Mines, Mine Detectors and Mine Eradicators

17. <u>Mines</u>. There is a requirement for improved non-metallic anti-vehicular and anti-personnel mines.

18. <u>Detection Devices</u>. No fully satisfactory method of rapid mine detection and removal now exists. The following types of mine detector and mine eradicator are required:

      a. A mine detector which is capable of detecting both metallic and non-metallic mines of all types, and which will overcome enemy counter-measures. The detector should be both portable and adaptable to vehicular mounting.

      b. Equipment which can travel cross-country and remove or detonate all mines in its path.

Infra-Red Equipment

19. There is a requirement in the various Arms and Services for devices employing infra-red rays, to increase the efficiency of night operations without sacrificing secrecy. These devices are for the following purposes:

      a. Area observation.

      b. Aiming of rifle, carbine, machine gun or other medium range, flat trajectory infantry weapons.

      c. Night driving of vehicles at at least 80% of normal daylight speeds.

      d. Night assembly of troops, particularly airborne units.

      e. Night surveying.

Miscellaneous

20. <u>Sketching Devices</u>. Development should be continued on automatic sketching devices similar to the present odograph and pedograph for use in reconnaissance work.

21. <u>Mine Detonation</u>. A requirement exists for an induction detonated firing device which will detonate a mine when a hostile mine detector is used in the mine field, and a remote control firing device which can be installed in a mine for use in laying controlled mine fields.

22. <u>Shaped Charges</u>. The present shaped demolition charges do not have sufficient power. A shaped charge powerful enough to penetrate 15 feet of reinforced concrete should be developed.

23. <u>Camouflage Materiel</u>. Existing camouflage nets absorb oil and water to the extent that their weight becomes excessive and when impregnated with oil constitute a fire hazard. Development should be undertaken to

produce camouflage materials which are resistant to absorption of oils and water and which are flameproof.

24. Air Compressor. A requirement exists for an air compressor of medium capacity but of light weight for use by airborne engineer and mountain engineer units.

25. Rock Crusher. An improved rock-crushing, screening, and washing plant is required to take care of increased demands for road construction materials in corps areas.

26. Surfacing Material. There is a requirement for an improved type of surfacing material which will carry divisional loads over all types of beach sand and similar soils. The development of this material should be coordinated with the Army Air Forces development of landing mats and soil stabilizing agents.

27. Prefabricated Buildings. There is a requirement for prefabricated buildings for such uses as hospital, shop, storage and administrative buildings. This development should be coordinated with the Army Air Forces' development of prefabricated buildings.

28. Searchlights. Development of searchlights should be continued to provide:

a. A light, portable searchlight suitable for battlefield illumination (artificial moonlight) and for use in coast artillery defense systems.

b. A fixed floodlight suitable for installation in casemates or turrets.

SECTION VIII

ARMORED AND TANK DESTROYER EQUIPMENT

General

1. Combat experiences in the recent war demonstrated that the principal missions of armor are to assist the Infantry in the assault and breakthrough, to exploit a breakthrough and to pursue the enemy. The tank, operating by direct fire and movement, is the armored striking element. Although the tank is capable of executing indirect artillery fire, such use is definitely a secondary mission.

2. In its original concept, the purpose of the tank destroyer was to place upon the battlefield a highly mobile and powerful antitank gun not then available in a tank. Whereas the typically thin-skinned highly gunned vehicle known as the tank destroyer will always be able to carry more powerful armament for the same overall weight than the corresponding tank, this inherent advantage does not justify the continuation of the development of this class of fighting vehicles in view of the present and future potentialities of tank armament, mobility and maneuverability. Therefore, development of the tank destroyer should be terminated.

3. The presence of armor on the battlefield always attracts enemy armor. It is imperative, therefore, that the tank class of weapons include one type of gun that is sufficiently powerful to knock out any weapon that the enemy may place upon the battlefield.

4. There should be no further development of towed antitank guns. The vulnerability of the gun crews to machine gun and artillery fire, together with the gun's lack of both mobility and ability to go into action promptly, mitigates against this type of weapon.

5. Future development of armored vehicles should be coordinated closely with the development of air transport, and where necessary, development of armor should include provisions for sectionalization, as well as the use of lighter, but equally tough metals in their construction so that all armored vehicles can be transported by air.

Tanks

6. In the development of a tank, first priority should be accorded to obtaining the prescribed firepower, maneuverability, and mobility, with armor protection a secondary, although important, consideration. The following general characteristics are applicable to all types of tanks: silent operation, including the track; excellent all-around vision; and built-in waterproofing with fording depth equal to the height of the tank.

7. Principal Types of Tanks. Three principal types of tanks are required to meet the needs of all branches for armor:

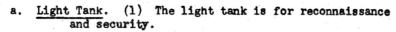

a. Light Tank. (1) The light tank is for reconnaissance and security.

    (2) The present light tank should be further developed to obtain the maximum firepower consistent with the maximum cross-country mobility and maneuverability and all-around armor protection against small arms and shell fragments, with frontal armor protection against light antitank guns. It should not exceed 25 tons in weight. The tank gun should be of approximately 3-inch caliber, capable of penetrating 5 inches of homogeneous armor at 30° obliquity at 1000 yards using special ammunition.

b. Medium Tank. (1) The medium tank is the principal weapon of armored divisions. It should be capable of assault action, exploitation, and pursuit. It is capable of serving in infantry antitank units, and when equipped with the 105mm howitzer should serve as the infantry cannon.

    (2) The present medium tank should be further developed stressing sustained action; great tactical and strategical mobility; all-around armor protection against light antitank guns, and frontal armor protection against medium antitank guns. Its weight should not exceed 45 tons. The gun should be of approximately 3-inch caliber, capable of penetrating 8 inches of homogeneous armor at 30° obliquity at 1000 yards using special ammunition.

c. Heavy Tank. (1) This tank should be developed for heavy assault action and breakthrough. It also should be capable of destroying any armored weapons that the enemy may place upon the battlefield, therefore, any conflicting requirements arising in future development as to gun size and destructiveness and mobility versus its armor protection should be resolved in favor of the gun and mobility.

    (2) The heavy tank should have superior firepower; possess superior tactical and excellent strategic mobility; and should be capable of safely traversing ordinary minefields and negotiating common obstacles. It should be very heavily armored, with front armor capable of withstanding any probable antitank fire, and should not exceed 75 tons in weight. The standard gun should be of approximately 90mm caliber, capable of penetrating 10 inches of homogeneous armor at 30° obliquity at 2000 yards using special ammunition.

The tank also should be capable of mounting a gun
of approximately 105mm caliber, capable of penetrating 10 inches of homogeneous armor at 30°
obliquity at 4000 yards using special ammunition.

8. **Special Tanks.** a. There is a requirement for a midget tank, weighing approximately twelve tons, to be used for limited range battlefield reconnaissance and in the initial phases of an airborne operation. This tank
should have the maximum cross-country mobility and maneuverability; should
be armed with automatic weapons capable of destroying personnel and lightly
armored vehicles; and should carry a crew of two men.

b. There is a requirement for an amphibious tank for use in ship
to shore operations; river crossings; on inland lakes, swamps, or rice paddies.
This tank should be capable of firing while moving in water and should be
capable of fighting on land for short periods of time.

c. There is a requirement for a special tank for engineer demolition work. This tank should be capable of carrying cargo and personnel, and
should be equipped with dozer blade, crane, mine detector, mine removing
attachment, and demolition launcher. Mobility and armor should be comparable
to that of the medium tank.

d. There is a requirement for a special flame throwing tank. See
Section XII, Chemical Warfare Equipment.

Tank Armament

9. **Tank Guns and Ammunition.** The following general characteristics
are desired in tank guns and ammunition:

a. Guns should be specifically designed with reference to the
space limitations in tanks, and with emphasis in obtaining:

(1) The shortest practicable chamber.

(2) The shortest distance from trunnion to breech block
that is consistent with a balanced turret.

(3) The shortest recoil with a compact recoil mechanism.

(4) A semiautomatic breech.

(5) Automatic loading with selective dual feeding of ammunition and capable of both electrical and mechanical
firing.

(6) Automatic gun fume scavenging.

b. Fixed Ammunition so crimped as to preclude accidental separation.
See Section XVI. Ammunition, for detailed discussion of tank ammunition.

c. Maximum backlash in elevating and traversing mechanism not to exceed $\frac{1}{4}$ mil.

d. Obscuration to be reduced to the absolute minimum.

e. Integrated fire control system incorporating:

(1) A stabilizer which will give horizontal and vertical stability to the tank gun during movement.

(2) A range finder integrated with a computing sight mechanism. The range finder should have 2% accuracy at 4000 yards and be operative by the gunner without his relinquishing the gun controls.

(3) A sight reticule capable of rapid change to correspond to the type of ammunition being used.

(4) An integrated joy-stick control for power traverse, elevation and firing. This should be capable of manual operation in an emergency.

10. <u>Machine Guns</u>. a. There should be developed a reliable .30 caliber machine gun capable of sustained fire at high cyclic rates, subject to minimum stoppages and designed for easy loading. This weapon will probably differ materially from the machine gun proposed in Section II, Infantry Equipment. This weapon should be capable of multiple mounting as follows:

(1) Inside the turret, coaxial with the tank gun.

(2) In ballistic blisters outside the turret, coaxial with the tank gun.

(3) As sponson guns, fired by the assistant driver using a parallelogram sight, or by remote control from the guns mounted in the ballistic blisters.

b. The machine gun finally adopted as the standard for antiaircraft use should be flexibly mounted on the turret for both antiaircraft and ground fire, capable of control by the tank commander through selective direct or remote means.

c. The coaxial machine gun mounts should provide for the installation of either the .30 caliber or the antiaircraft machine gun.

11. <u>Tank-borne Rocket Launchers</u>. There is a requirement for a rocket launcher which can be mounted on tanks without interfering with the other tank armament. This launcher should be capable of being loaded without exposure of the crew.

12. **Auxiliary Flame Thrower.** There is a requirement for a swivel type flame thrower, for mounting in the roof of the assistant driver's compartment, which is capable of accurate laying and of lateral traverse within the limits of vision of the assistant driver. The flame thrower should provide 100 seconds of fire and possess the maximum range obtainable. Installation should be possible by field ordnance units.

Tank Components and Accessories

13. **Tank Components.** The design of tanks has reached a phase where development of more efficient components, such as power plant, tracks and drive, is essential to enable the necessary mobility, maneuverability and gun mounting to be attained within reasonable overall dimensions and weight.

    a. Special engines should be developed for tanks and other heavy, self-propelled equipment in stages of approximately 500, 1000, and 1500 horsepower. Development should investigate multi-fuel engines, turbines and combination internal combustion engine-electric power plants.

    b. There is a requirement for two types of tracks: a training and strategic movement track designed to prevent damage to roads, and a combat track equipped for attachable ice cleats or special traction and flotation devices.

    c. Development of armor should endeavor to obtain greater protection with reduced weights. Armor must be developed to provide greater protection from shaped charges and armor piercing projectiles. The use of alloys, plastics, spaced plates, and hedgehog spikes and laminated construction should be investigated. Angular placement of armor giving sloped surfaces should be studied with a view to securing additional protection.

14. **Amphibian Kits.** Kits should be developed for all armored vehicles which will enable the vehicle to engage in any amphibious operation without interference with the standard weapons of the vehicle. The kit must be suitable for use in either fresh or salt water in motion.

15. **Climatic Kits.** Kits should be developed which will permit vehicular and weapon operation at extremes of temperature and humidity, while at the same time providing for the comfort of the crew to insure efficient crew performance. The kits should be applicable from minus 10° to minus 40°, and from plus 120° to plus 140°, with due consideration being given to winds up to 40 mph.

16. **Remote Control Device.** There is a requirement for a remote control device capable of controlling the steering, speed and firing of track and wheeled vehicles when used as decoys, targets, or as reconnaissance agents. The device should be capable of rapid installation and removal in the field, without necessitating extensive modification of the vehicle.

17. **Periscopic Sight.** A periscopic sight should be developed to assist in preventing obscuration in tanks and for use with defiladed self-propelled

howitzers in order to permit them to execute an emergency role of direct fire with HEAT ammunition against enemy tanks.

18. <u>Mine Remover</u>. There is a requirement for a mechanism, to be used in the engineer demolition tank and selected tanks within a tank battalion, which will detect and remove or detonate mines.

19. <u>Local Defense Weapon</u>. There is a requirement for a weapon to cover the dead space around a tank from individuals armed with shaped charges. Such a weapon might employ high explosives or chemicals. Chemicals, if used, should also provide instantaneous smoke clouds for concealment and movement.

Auxiliary Vehicles

20. <u>Light, Partially Armored Truck</u>. There is a requirement for a light, wheeled, partially armored truck of the approximate size of the present $\frac{1}{4}$-ton truck for use by reconnaissance elements; and by commanders, liaison officers and others whose duties require them to be habitually mounted in exposed vehicles. This vehicle should provide side armor and partial overhead armor capable of protecting against small arms fire and shell fragments. Maximum cross-country capabilities, motive power, traction and flotation approaching that of the current $\frac{1}{4}$-ton truck are desired. Provision should be included for mounting a .50 caliber machine gun, radio, and for carrying a crew of three men. The $\frac{1}{4}$-ton truck, 6x6, formerly under development as an ambulance, should be investigated in this development.

21. <u>Full Track Armored Carriers</u>. There is a requirement for full track armored personnel carriers to transport personnel or vital cargo over fire-swept areas. Two carriers, one of 26-man capacity and the other of 12-man capacity, should be developed. The carriers should possess the maximum interchangeability of parts and should provide armor protection from small arms fire and shell fragments. An armored top is essential. With minimum rearrangement of the interior, these carriers should be adapted for use as mortar carriers, armored command post vehicles or armored observation post tenders to meet the needs of all Arms.

22. <u>Tank Transporter</u>. Two tank transporters should be developed. One should be capable of carrying the heavy tank and the other the medium tank. Both transporters should be capable of carrying general cargo of the equivalent weight of the tanks.

23. <u>Heavy Recovery Vehicles</u>. Two types of heavy recovery vehicles, with armor protection for the operating personnel against small arms and shell fragments, should be developed for battlefield evacuation of tanks and other tracked equipment. One type should be capable of evacuating heavy and medium tanks, the other medium and light tanks. Both recovery vehicles should be so designed as to be capable of evacuating other type vehicles of comparable weight.

24. **Tank-drawn Infantry Sleds.** There is a requirement for an armored, low silhouette sled, for carrying infantry over fire-swept areas, which can be towed by tanks. Armor should provide protection from small arms fire and partial protection from artillery air bursts.

25. **Special Bridging Equipment.** There is a requirement for two bridges which can be carried, placed, and released by an armored vehicle without exposure of personnel: one to carry the light and medium tanks over 40-foot spans; and the other to carry the medium and heavy tanks over 60 to 80-foot spans. See Section VII, Engineer Equipment.

26. **Tank Dozer.** A dozer blade, capable of being used on all types of tanks, should be developed. Such a blade should be capable of easy installation and removal and should not interfere with the mobility or weapons of the tank.

Communications and Radar Equipment

27. **Communication Equipment.** There is a requirement for the following communications equipment, the details of which will be found in Section XVII, Communications Equipment:

a. An integrated air-ground voice radio suitable for mounting in armored vehicles and capable of communication with the several Arms.

b. Television equipment for target observation for artillery, information for commanders and identification between units.

c. Small, compact, mechanical authenticating devices providing simple and rapid authentication.

d. Speech security equipment for voice communication over radio or telephone.

e. Page facsimile equipment as a rapid means of transmitting sketches, overlays, and enemy information.

f. Modulated light beam equipment as another channel of communication.

g. Small, portable radio to provide communication between dismounted men and tanks.

h. Two-way communications equipment in all tanks.

i. Directional antennas to minimize hostile interceptions.

j. A simplified method of radio set alignment.

28. **Radar Equipment.** There is a requirement for the following radar equipment, the details of which will be found in Section XIX, Radar Equipment:

a. Means of detecting moving or stationary ground targets.

b. Means of accurate target identification, range determination, automatic tracking, computation of lead and gun laying.

c. A precise, non-magnetic, navigational (homing) instrument for use in tanks and other armored vehicles.

d. Equipment which will insure positive automatic identification between aircraft, armored vehicles and other ground troops.

Miscellaneous Equipment

29. Clothing. Clothing of armored personnel should be comfortable, fire-resistant, and facilitate entering, leaving, and fighting in armored vehicles. One-piece suits, field jackets, trousers, hoods, combat boots and tank helmets should be especially designed to meet this requirement.

30. Gas Protection. There is a requirement for the collective protection of tank crews from both noxious gases and chemical agents.

31. Night Attack Aids. There should be developed aids to facilitate night attack by Armor through improvement of night vision aids, sights and fire control equipment. Investigation in the fields of optical equipment, infra-red, radar and artificial illumination is indicated.

32. Deception Aids. Research and development in the fields of sound, camouflage and radio deception are needed to produce aids which will deceive the enemy in both day and night armored operations.

33. Target Indicator. There is a requirement for a devise by means of which front line troops can accurately designate targets to Armor.

34. Tank Maps. Development of tank maps should be initiated to show types and consistencies of soil under varying meteorological conditions, and to indicate terrain passable and impassable to tanks. See Section VII, Engineer Equipment.

35. Aircraft. There is a requirement in armored units for light organic aircraft for use in reconnaissance, control, courier service and fire adjustment. These aircraft should be of either the light airplane or helicopter type. For a detailed discussion, see Section XI, Air Support Equipment.

36. Blast Mats. Improved blast mats are required for minimizing obscuration of sight in emplaced positions.

SECTION IX

MEDICAL EQUIPMENT

General

1. Field medical equipment should retain all of the technical efficiency of fixed equipment, but at the same time should be capable of being quickly knocked-down, folded or packed, transported and re-assembled without resultant damage. All items should be capable of being transported by air.

2. Utilization of light helicopter aircraft for the evacuation of casualties from forward areas, development of which is provided herein, may enable major reorganization of the methods, equipment and channels of evacuation. The goal to be sought is the evacuation of the wounded from the most advanced collecting point direct to the Evacuation Hospital, or similar installation, and special emphasis should be placed on this development.

3. The Armored Medical Research Laboratory at Fort Knox, Kentucky, conducts projects Army-wide in scope and therefore should be retained under the direct control of The Surgeon General.

4. Research should be continued to evolve methods for promoting psychological warfare applicable to all ground troops and to develop equipment therefor, including the following:

    a. The mental conditioning necessary to prepare a man psychologically for combat.

    b. The rehabilitation of casualties.

    c. The prevention and treatment of battle fatigue.

    d. The physical and psychological factors involved in the operation of weapons and equipment under all conditions.

    e. The offensive phase of psychological warfare, such as the ways and means of destroying the enemy's morale and will to fight.

Ambulances

5. The present standard 3/4-ton knock-down type ambulance has demonstrated outstanding suitability and should be retained. Provision should be made for blackout and the heating, cooling, and ventilation facilities should be improved.

6. A small ambulance with knock-down type body, low silhouette and good cross-country mobility is required for evacuation of casualties from

the most forward battalion aid stations and over difficult terrain. A $\frac{1}{4}$-ton 6x6 type ambulance chassis should be developed for that purpose.

7. a. A flying ambulance of the helicopter type is required to remove casualties from front-line units located in very difficult terrain. The flying ambulance should be organic equipment of appropriate medical units. See Section XI, Air Support Equipment.

b. The present policy of utilizing standard transport aircraft, suitably modified and operated by Army Air Forces, for air evacuation from rear areas has proven satisfactory and should be continued.

Special Purpose Vehicle Bodies

8. The present bodies on the standard $2\frac{1}{2}$-ton truck chassis are satisfactory for the following special purpose vehicles; however, improvement of the bodies should keep pace with new developments:

    a. Optical repair truck.

    b. Dental operating truck.

    c. Dental laboratory truck.

    d. Medical laboratory truck.

Equipment

9. **Kits.** a. The various kits listed below appear to be satisfactory in their present forms. However, most of the kits have been recently developed and have not undergone extended service tests. If, as a result of these service tests, any of the kits prove unsatisfactory, development should be continued to produce a satisfactory model. In addition, all kits will require continued study and revision to conform to the advance of medical science.

    (1) Kit, medical.

        (a) Medical Officers.

        (b) Medical NCO's.

        (c) Medical Privates.

        (d) Dental Officers.

        (e) Veterinary Officers.

    (2) Kit, first aid.

    (3) Kit, first aid, jungle.

(4) Kit, first aid, vehicle.

(5) Kit, first aid, combat vehicle.

(6) Kit, first aid, gas casualty, individual.

(7) Kit, water testing, screening, chemical agents.

(8) Kit, water testing, poisons, treatment control.

b. The kit, medical, parachute, is not satisfactory since the equipment in it is frequently broken on landing. This kit should be redesigned.

10. <u>Chest</u>. A standard chest is required for Medical Department assemblies. Insofar as practicable the chest and its contents should not exceed a load of 50 pounds. The present assemblies are in need of reorganization on a more purely functional basis and a separate chest, packed for combat alone, is desirable.

11. <u>Packing Box</u>. A standard reusable packing box for medical supplies should be developed. The box and contents should not exceed a one-man load.

12. <u>Litters</u>. Litters should be constructed of the lightest practicable materials to prevent excessive fatigue of the litter bearers. The present straight aluminum litter is satisfactory. The folding litter is not sturdy enough for field usage and should be made with stronger joints.

13. <u>Packboard</u>. A lightweight packboard with a water resistant carrier, suitably partitioned to carry medical supplies, is required for infantry and mountain divisions.

14. <u>Folding Bed</u>. A lightweight, rugged, folding, hospital-type bed is required for use by field medical units to replace the canvas folding cot which is uncomfortable and too low for proper treatment of the patients. It should be equipped with a lightweight mattress.

15. <u>Blankets</u>. a. A lightweight, water resistant, olive drab colored blanket which will provide maximum warmth is required for field use.

b. A more attractively colored, lightweight, warm blanket would be a psychological asset in wards of mobile field hospitals and should be developed.

16. <u>Folding Dental Chair</u>. The present folding field dental chair is too heavy and inflexible. A new lightweight chair should be developed with an electric dental motor and a foot pedal for emergency use.

17. **Field Oxygen Therapy Apparatus.** Present apparatus is too heavy and cumbersome. New apparatus should permit two or more patients to be fed from one source of supply and incorporate maximum safety and simplicity of operation with economy of weight and cubage.

18. **Oxygen Generating Apparatus.** At present, field hospital units are dependent for resupply upon oxygen in high pressure cylinders. There is a need for a lightweight, mobile generating apparatus which can efficiently supply the needs of these field medical units.

19. **Field Instrument Sterilizer.** The range of sizes and general features of design of the present sterilizer are satisfactory. Unsatisfactory performance has been due to the use of substitute materials in lieu of corrosion resisting metal.

20. **Portable Field Suction Apparatus.** The present equipment should be made lighter and smaller.

21. **Field X-ray Unit and Accessories.** There should be a comprehensive study of all X-ray equipment specifically designed for field use with a view to making it smaller and lighter without loss of ruggedness.

22. **Housing Facilities.** Present canvas tents have not proven satisfactory. Lightweight canvas or prefabricated housing, which will provide improved protection for the sick and wounded and for technical medical equipment, should be developed for aid stations, wards and operating rooms of field medical units. Where practicable, light sectional flooring should be provided for operating rooms, X-ray rooms and dental clinics.

23. **Heating Units.** Lighter weight, more efficient units should be developed for heating field operating rooms, wards and aid stations.

24. **Generators.** Inasmuch as the demand is for more and more electrified equipment, heavy duty generators are required which will provide sufficient power and reliability for operation 24 hours per day.

25. **Portable Electric Lantern.** Present gasoline lanterns are unreliable and do not provide adequate light. A portable electric lantern should be developed which will provide satisfactory lighting for aid stations which have no generators and for auxiliary, emergency lighting in field hospitals.

26. **Water Supply Equipment.** A lightweight, durable water storage and distribution system, with provision for showers, should be developed. In addition, a stable drug which will rapidly sterilize contaminated water for drinking purposes, without imparting an offensive taste to the water, is required.

27. **Washing Machine.** Field hospital units should be provided with a simple, lightweight washing machine for use when laundry facilities are not available.

28. <u>Baking Facilities</u>. Present field stoves should be improved so that they can provide baked goods and pastries of high nutritive value for medical patients.

29. <u>Insecticides and Insect Repellants</u>. An insecticide is required which is toxic to all insect vectors of disease and insect pests, without being toxic to man, animal, food or water. An insect repellant should be developed that is non-irritating to skin, eyes and mucous membranes, non-injurious to clothing and equipment, and non-offensive to smell and taste, which will effectively prevent bites by mosquitoes, mites, ticks and other insects.

30. <u>Contact Eye Lenses</u>. Contact eye lenses should be provided for use by combat troops with faulty vision.

31. New models of the following items have been recently developed. They appear to satisfy present requirements, although extended service tests may reveal a need for further development:

    a. Portable field autoclave.

    b. Field operating lamp.

    c. Field operating table.

    d. Field scrub sink.

    e. Small field refrigerator.

SECTION X

AIRBORNE EQUIPMENT

General

1. The greatly increased use of airborne operations is envisioned for the next war. In such operations it should be the responsibility of the Army Air Forces to deliver preparatory fires on the landing areas prior to the landing; to transport, convoy, and land the troops and equipment; to furnish fire support during and after landing; and to provide continuous resupply.

2. The feasibility of conducting an airborne ship to shore operation should be investigated.

3. Airborne divisions should be capable of sustained action in combat equivalent to that of an infantry division; therefore, units of the airborne division should utilize weapons and equipment standard for equivalent components of an infantry division. Certain additional items of special equipment will be required for paratroopers.

4. All of the equipment of standard infantry and airborne divisions and all other ground force equipment, except the very heaviest items, should be air transportable. The aircraft developed to carry this equipment should include cargo carrying transport airplanes and both the assault and cargo type gliders. To attain this air transportability, a balanced compromise between ground force equipment and aircraft design should be achieved in the development phase by coordination between Army Ground Forces and Army Air Forces.

Aircraft

5. <u>Gliders</u>. There are requirements for a 4-ton assault glider and a cargo glider having the largest capacity obtainable. These gliders should be of all metal construction and should provide rear loading. The towing of gliders should be accomplished by standard aircraft, therefore, the development of gliders should be coordinated with development of aircraft capable of performing towing missions.

6. <u>Helicopters</u>. There is a requirement for a cargo helicopter to assist in the supply of airborne troops and for use in ship to shore operations. This helicopter should be designed for use as a flying crane, and continuing development should provide the largest weight lift capacity possible.

7. <u>Transport Aircraft</u>. There are requirements for 10-ton and 50-ton cargo carrying aircraft. Development of these planes should provide for mass parachute jumping, glider towing, self-sealing gas tanks, readily removable armor protection for occupants and engines, and the

loading and unloading of self-propelled equipment operating under its own power. These aircraft should be capable of utilizing hastily constructed airfields.

Auxiliary Equipment

8. Parachutes. There are requirements for improved personnel and cargo parachutes. The personnel parachute must provide for use from high speed airplanes, damping out oscillation, and quick release means. The cargo parachutes must provide for the dropping of loads up to 5000 pounds either by the use of a single parachute or by the use of a series of parachutes.

9. Containers. There are requirements for parachute, free fall, and large size types of containers. Parachute containers should be shock resistant, provide for delayed opening of the parachute and capable of being aimed and dropped from a high altitude in a controlled pattern. Free fall containers must provide for the accurate and safe dropping of the more rugged items of equipment and supply. The large size container should be capable of single or combination fit into bomb bays or cargo compartments. These large size containers must be so shaped as to utilize the maximum capacity of the airplane.

10. Cargo Jettisoning Device. There are requirements for more efficient cargo jettisoning devices. Roller conveyor systems and a control device which will permit the simultaneous ejection of personnel and cargo from a formation of aircraft should be developed.

11. Personnel Exits. There is a requirement for a more rapid means of exit from aircraft for paratroopers. Development should examine the use of multiple doors or the ejection from the plane of containers carrying groups of men.

12. Navigational Aids. There is a requirement for a navigational aid employing a fixed base behind friendly lines which will give pinpoint accuracy in locating the drop or landing zones.

13. Communications. There are requirements for improved communications for use in airborne operations. Development should provide improved air to ground communication equipment and long range equipment which will enable an airborne unit to contact its rear base of operations. See Section XVII, Communication Equipment.

14. Vehicle Flying Kits. The feasibility of developing kits which will convert tanks, armored cars, trucks, and weasel type vehicles into gliders should be investigated.

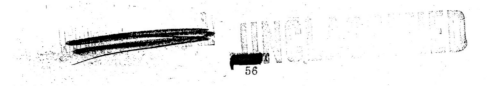

AIR SUPPORT EQUIPMENT

General

1. Air support is air power employed in direct furtherance of the ground effort of a particular command. Air support missions include air reconnaissance beyond the capabilities of the ground commander, securing control of the air above the supported ground unit, and fire support against ground targets by means of weapons mounted on or carried by aircraft.

2. Fire support by air weapons should be available against enemy aviation overhead and against ground targets interfering with the ground force mission whenever the air situation permits. However, high performance air reconnaissance is required by ground elements regardless of the status of the air battle. The characteristics of air fire power make necessary careful integration of such fire power with the fire plan of the ground front as a whole, and provision for extensive liaison and communications facilities between ground and air commands concerned.

3. Air support missions involving the use of high performance aircraft, in general, should remain a responsibility of the Army Air Forces.

4. The Army Ground Forces should be provided with organic light aircraft capable of providing limited observation and transportation and of operating from small unprepared landing strips in forward areas.

Organic Army Ground Forces Aviation

5. Infantry, Cavalry, Field Artillery and Armored Units, and various command echelons and installations from Division to Army, require organic light aircraft, operated by Army Ground Forces personnel, for the accomplishment of the following missions:

    a. Close-in observation.

    b. Battlefield reconnaissance, both visual and electronic.

    c. Adjustment of fire of short range field artillery, rockets and guided missiles.

    d. Control and liaison.

    e. Local courier and messenger service.

    f. Limited aerial photography.

    g. Individual and group transportation, evacuation of casualties and emergency supply within the combat area.

6. Types of Aircraft. The following aircraft are required:

a. Light liaison aircraft, both fixed wing and rotary wing types. These aircraft should be of the lightest practicable weight consistent with all metal construction. Design should stress simplicity, to reduce pilotage and maintenance problems, and capability of operation from small unprepared strips, with two to three hours endurance at 80 to 95 mph. Consideration should be given to the feasibility of a design, such as folding wings, which also will enable the aircraft to be driven on highways as a vehicle.

b. Two or three place liaison aircraft, both fixed wing and rotary wing types. General characteristics of these aircraft should be the same as for the light liaison aircraft listed in a above, but endurance at cruising speed should be $3\frac{1}{2}$ to 4 hours.

c. (1) Transport aircraft, 1000-2000 pound payload, both fixed wing and rotary wing types.

(2) Transport aircraft, 2000-6000 pound payload, both fixed wing and rotary wing types. Endurance of these aircraft should be four hours, with two hours the minimum acceptable. All weather operation is desirable. These aircraft should be convertible to cargo, passenger or ambulance use.

Aircraft Organic to the Army Air Forces

7. Missions of the Army Air Forces in providing air support to the Army Ground Forces include:

a. Denial of the combat area to hostile aircraft and screening from hostile observation the area occupied by friendly troops.

b. Collection of information by visual, photographic and electronic means.

c. Destruction or neutralization of all types of ground targets capable of affecting the operation of the Ground Forces.

d. Adjustment of long range fires beyond the capabilities of the organic means of ground troops.

e. Support of ground operations by providing transportation for airborne troops, supply and evacuation.

8. Types of Aircraft. The following types of aircraft are required for the support of ground operations:

a. Tactical reconnaissance types, to provide visual, tactical and electronic reconnaissance and to adjust long range fire.

b. Fire support types, for use of the Army Air Forces in the

destruction or neutralization of hostile forces, activities and installations affecting the current operation of the ground command.

  c. Transportation types, to carry airborne troop units and their equipment and supplies, and to effect strategic supply movements in rear areas and from rear areas to the combat area.

  d. Photographic types, detailed discussion of which is contained in Section VII, Engineer Equipment.

  9. <u>Design</u>. The following considerations should influence the design of all aircraft intended for use by the Army Air Forces in cooperation with the Army Ground Forces:

  a. Maximum visibility for the air crew.

  b. Accurate and reliable means for navigation, positioning, target designation, front line identification and delivery of destructive power in all weather conditions and at night.

  c. Fast and reliable means for communication and control between the aircraft and ground or airborne controlling stations.

  d. Operation from air fields with minimum of preparation forward of the Army rear boundary.

Electronic Equipment

  10. <u>Radio</u>. Requirements exist for the following, the details of which are set forth in Section XVII, Communication Equipment:

  a. Lighter weight, more reliable radio sets for communication between ground control and cooperating aircraft.

  b. Voice scrambling devices for security.

  c. Facsimile equipment for transmission of air photos, maps, overlays, etc.

  d. Improvements are needed in existing communication means to obtain smaller, lighter, more portable equipment providing an integrated, all weather, faster and more reliable system for use between ground stations and between ground and air.

  e. Teletypewriters for rapid, reliable communication between ground control, airdromes and aircraft in flight.

  f. Radio relay equipment enabling small portable equipment in the front line to communicate directly with ground aircraft stations and with cooperating aircraft.

11. Radar. Requirements exist for the following, the details of which are discussed in Section XIX, Radar Equipment:

a. Smaller, lighter, more mobile and longer range radar sets whose received image is comparable in quality to television and capable of reproduction for later detailed study.

b. Counter radar equipment to include a paint or coating for aircraft which will not reflect radar pulse.

12. Television. Requirements exist for the following, details of which are covered in Section XVIII, Survey, Observation and Meteorological Equipment:

a. Lightweight, highly mobile television equipment for reconnaissance, target designation and control of aircraft and air weapons in flight and for supplementing air photography.

b. Combination of electronic equipment enabling a commander to view critical points in his battle area, to communicate directly with subordinates there and with other elements including cooperating aviation.

c. Means for permanently reproducing screen images of high fidelity for later detailed study.

d. Simple, lightweight devices carried by ground forces and activated by them or from the air which will indicate on television picture their location on the terrain being televised.

Miscellaneous Equipment

13. Bombsighting. Need exists for improved bombsighting equipment and means for accurately guiding bombs.

14. Target Marking. Improved means for marking targets and of indicating lines short of which bombing and air attacks will not take place are needed.

15. Identification Means. Positive means and methods for identifying friendly vehicles and aircraft and the location of front line troops should be developed.

SECTION XII

CHEMICAL WARFARE EQUIPMENT

General

1. Toxic chemical and biological agents were not used in the past war. Fear of reprisal by an opponent more ably equipped to wage chemical warfare was the deterrent to the use of chemicals by Germany and Japan. For the purposes of development of equipment it must be assumed that chemicals will be used in any future war. Therefore, research and development of chemical and biological agents should be continuous.

Chemical and Biological Agents

2. Recent discoveries have produced new chemical and biological agents of astounding lethal or destructive potentialities. To achieve full strategical and tactical value therefrom, methods of dissemination of these agents over large areas should be evolved and perfected. Progress to date indicates a probability of the discovery of even more powerful lethal agents, and research should be directed to that end.

3. The provision of countermeasures for all known chemical and biological agents requires imaginative and diligent development to the end that the civil population, as well as the military, shall be educated in and provided with means for detection of, and protection from, such agents.

Protective Equipment

4. The recent development of new chemical and biological agents has rendered all of the present protective equipment ineffective. Development of protective equipment must keep pace with the development of new agents. The following equipment is required:

    a. Combat Gas Mask. Emphasis should be given to providing protection against all toxic agents, reducing weight and increasing the flexibility of the face piece. The mask should have a waterproof carrier suitable for amphibious use.

    b. Protective Clothing. Protective clothing is required which is suitable for continuous wear and which provides maximum protection against chemical agents. If practicable, the clothing should also be flameproof and afford protection against biological agents, insects and radio-active materials. Consideration should be given to the incorporation of protective

characteristics into the cloth at the time of manufacture.

c. Protective Ointment. Protective ointment should be developed concurrently with the development of new agents.

d. Collective Protector. A light, mobile, collective protector is required to provide a shelter in a gassed area where the soldier can remove his gas mask and adjust his equipment. Development of collective protectors for tanks, telephone exchanges, aid stations, hospitals, and command posts should be continued to provide a longer period of protection, better ventilation and reduction in bulk and weight of the equipment.

e. Shoe Impregnite. Waterproofing qualities should be combined with an improved shoe impregnite which will give protection against new chemical agents.

f. Detectors. (1) A simple detector kit should be developed concurrently with the development of new agents, as such agents may be colorless, tasteless and odorless.

(2) Treated paint and paper type detectors should be improved to detect any new liquid vesicants.

g. Dust Respirator. A light, expendable respirator which affords maximum protection from dust should be developed.

h. Eyeshield. The present eyeshield should be improved to provide a scratch-resistant, anti-fogging, anti-glare lens and to reduce irritation caused by the velvet edging.

i. Animal Protective Equipment. Protective masks and goggles and protective ointment should be provided for animals. See Section III, Cavalry Equipment.

Weapons and Ammunition

5. Chemical Mortars. 4.2-inch or 105mm mortar. Only one mortar of this general caliber should be developed. It should combine the best features of the present 4.2-inch chemical mortar and the 105mm mortar, and be suitable for firing chemical projectiles. See Section II, Infantry Equipment.

6. Ammunition. a. Projectiles. Chemical, biological, smoke, incendiary and flame fillings should be developed for projectiles of all weapons of suitable calibers and types. In addition to chemical and biological fillings, the following special projectiles should be developed:

(1) A high explosive-toxic projectile, not distinguishable on detonation from a normal high explosive projectile.

(2) An incendiary-toxic shell.

(3) An illuminating shell with one minute or more burning time and illumination of approximately 200,000 candlepower.

(4) An improved incendiary, flame and anti-personnel projectile of the jelled gasoline type.

(5) An improved smoke projectile with better obscuring qualities.

(6) A smoke projectile which will obscure from both visual and radar observation.

(7) A projectile filling which provides an effective radar countermeasure.

b. Fuzes. (1) The VT fuze should be standardized for use with chemical loads in all types of projectiles.

(2) A combination super-quick and delay fuze and a combination super-quick and time fuze should be developed for use with chemical projectiles.

c. Grenades. All types of chemical-filled grenades require improvement. Signalling and marking grenades should have stronger colored smokes and should have the optimum burning time.

Flame Throwers

7. Research should continue on methods of projecting flame more efficiently to greater ranges. This development will probably require marked departures from present methods of projecting flame. However, pending the development of new methods and equipment, the present equipment should be improved. Types of equipment required are as follows:

a. Portable Flame Throwers. (1) The present portable flame thrower should be improved by increasing the range, accuracy, and fuel capacity, reducing the weight, lowering the silhouette and adding safety features.

(2) The manifold type flame thrower should be improved and simplified.

(3) Development of the one-shot portable flame thrower, using burning cordite for pressure, should be continued to produce a low cost, expendable flame thrower with maximum capacity and range.

      (4) A new type portable flame thrower which will fire
cartridges of jelled gasoline or other semi-solid
fuel in a slow burning envelope should be developed.

  b. **Mechanized Flame Throwers.** (1) The present tank
mounted flame throwers should be improved to provide increased range and fuel capacity.

      (2) There is a requirement for a special flame throw-
ing tank to execute missions beyond the capabilities of tanks equipped with present small, auxiliary flame throwers. A pump operated model should
be developed as the principal weapon of a standard
tank. This flame thrower should provide the maximum range and fuel capacity obtainable.

  c. **Fuels.** There is a need for great improvement of flame thrower
fuels, including development of fortified, metallized and self-igniting fuels.
Research should be continued on the use of jelled toxic fuels.

  d. **Servicing Kits.** Kits should have increased simplicity and ra-
pidity of operation in mixing fuel and charging flame thrower fuel tanks.

  e. **Beach Defense Equipment.** Study should be continued of oil line
systems for the employment of incendiary oil in wall-of-flame beach defenses.

Smoke and Incendiary Equipment

  8. **Smoke Generators.** a. **Mechanical.** The mechanical smoke generator
should be made more mobile, rugged and reliable.

  b. **Combustion Type.** This type generator should be developed for
mounting in airplanes for use in covering high points on the ground not usual-
ly covered by ground screens.

  c. **Airplane Spray Tanks.** These tanks should have larger capacities
and the technique of spray distribution of smoke and chemicals should be improved.

  d. **Smoke Pots.** Smoke pots should be stable and non-toxic, and
should produce much less flare than present models.

  9. **Incendiary Devices.** a. An incendiary delay device should be perfected for the destruction of documents.

  b. Various types of incendiary sabotage devices should be developed.

SECTION XIII

FREE ROCKETS

General

1. In the recent war the use of field artillery type free rockets, because of their short range and large dispersion, was limited to that of special purpose weapons firing crash concentrations on large areas. The present status of rocket development indicates that both range and accuracy can be improved to a point where the rocket could be used profitably, in lieu of artillery or bombing, on missions requiring saturation of area targets.

2. Free rockets, compared to conventional field artillery weapons, possess inherent advantages of utilizing relatively light, highly mobile launchers, high percentage of filler in relation to projectile weight and production of a large mass of fire in a very short period of time. However, the prospects for improvement in the flexibility and accuracy of rockets, to a degree equivalent to conventional field artillery of the light and medium calibers, are not sufficiently promising at this time to warrant any assumption that the rocket eventually will replace all conventional field artillery weapons.

3. To achieve the ultimate utilization of rockets envisaged herein, much intensive basic research will be necessary. Initially the development of production models should be subordinated to such research. When basic research reaches a stage where development of a production model rocket is warranted, priority of development should be accorded the smallest caliber rocket listed herein because of the relatively lower outlay of funds involved for a small caliber rocket. Once the basic problems are solved, the principles can be applied to other rockets.

4. .The basic research program should investigate methods of obtaining: a projectile of optimum ballistics in flight; increased stability of the rocket while it is being accelerated; improved propellant, to include reducing its sensitivity to temperature extremes; safe transportation and storage; and an accurate rocket-assisted artillery projectile to achieve very long range. The program should include the following rockets:

    a. Field Artillery rockets.

    b. Special purpose rockets.

    c. Bazooka type rockets. See Section II, Infantry Equipment.

Field Artillery Rockets

5. Development of a group of free rockets, covering ranges up to 45,000 yards and possessing the greatest obtainable flexibility and accuracy, should

be considered. The following military characteristics are presented only as a guide and should in no way restrict research and development. To allow maximum freedom in securing optimum ballistic design, the size of the rocket, in the following tables, is stated in weight of head rather than in caliber.

6. <u>Gun Type Rockets</u>. The following rockets should be developed to supplement field artillery cannon, particularly in situations requiring rapid saturation of area targets:

Weight of Head (Payload)(lbs)	Maximum Range (Yds)	Accuracy and Destructive Effect Comparable to
* 30 - 35	13,000	105mm howitzer
90 - 100	25,000	155mm gun
200	45,000	8-inch gun

*Recommended for priority of development.

7. <u>Mortar Type Rockets</u>. The following rockets are required to provide short range, heavy demolitions and all weather close support comparable to close-in air bombardment:

Weight of Head (Payload)(lbs)	Maximum Range (Yds)
250	10,000
500	12,000
1000	15,000

Special Purpose Rockets

8. The rocket is particularly suitable for a number of special purposes involving the need for motive power or of a large capacity head for special loadings. Special purpose rockets should be included in the rocket development program, as indicated below.

9. <u>Chemical Rocket</u>. The feasibility of utilizing rockets for the dissemination of chemical and biological agents should be investigated.

10. <u>Antiaircraft Rocket</u>. A high velocity rocket, of improved fragmentation and utilizing the VT fuze, should be developed for use against low-flying aircraft of the Kamikaze type.

11. <u>Prime Mover Rockets</u>. Methods of transporting wire, cables, mine clearing devices, and other articles for short distances by the utilization of free rockets as prime movers should be continually improved to correspond with improved rocket performance.

12. <u>Illuminating Rockets</u>. Illuminating rockets should be developed to meet the requirement of Infantry, Armor, Field Artillery and Coast Artillery, with the minimum practicable number of types.

Launchers, Fuzes and Ammunition

13. <u>Rocket Launchers</u>. Development should be coordinated with that of free rockets. To obtain flexibility in tactical employment, research and development should include towed and self-propelled multiple tube launchers, single and multiple crate type launchers, single tube launchers capable of being man-handled and automatic type launchers. The following goals should be sought in the development of multiple tube launchers:

a. Insofar as practicable, the same carriage should be used for all calibers of rockets. Carriages should be equipped with interchangeable and removable clusters.

b. Launchers should be simple, rugged, possess good cross-country mobility and be able to withstand overseas shipment. Towed launchers should be of minimum practicable weight. In designing the towed rocket launcher, it should be assumed that rockets will not be habitually transported in the launcher tubes.

c. Better heat dissipation should be obtained to permit prompter reloading.

14. <u>Fuzes</u>. Standard artillery fuzes, including VT types, should be used with free rockets where practicable.

15. <u>Ammunition</u>. The capabilities of free rockets as fragmentation, demolition, smoke and chemical projectiles should be determined. The use of the VT fuze in conjunction with the fragmentation and chemical type projectiles should be investigated.

SECTION XIV

GUIDED MISSILES

General

1. The success of the guided missiles used during the late war indicates that weapons of this class will play a prominent role in future warfare. These missiles will attain supersonic speeds; travel at very high altitudes; and will be guided to the target by remote electronic control, self-contained "memory" devices, or homing devices attracted to heat, sound or metals. Intercontinental missiles, capable of carrying atomic explosive over ranges in excess of 3,000 miles, are probable within the predictable future.

2. The early detection of hostile guided missiles may require warning or detector stations to be far removed from the launching sites of friendly interceptor missiles in order to assure timely warning and due to the fact that radar possesses the inherent limitation of line-of-sight projection that is not effective below the horizon. Therefore, fire direction and control and detector facilities for antiaircraft defense should be expanded on an equal priority with the development of antiaircraft guided missiles.

3. This country lacks experience in the field of guided missiles. It is mandatory that basic research be continued to obtain the optimum ballistics, propellants and methods of guidance. There must be an integrated program to correlate the efforts of the various scientific groups engaged in research in the fields of ballistics, propulsion and guiding devices. Establishment of close liaison between those responsible for the development of nuclear energy and those engaged in the development of guided missiles is imperative in order to utilize atomic explosives in the warheads of the missiles.

Uses of Guided Missiles

4. The uses, and tentative military characteristics, that can be foreseen for guided missiles at the present time are:

    a. Antiaircraft Guided Missile. To effect a high probability of destroying maneuvering aircraft flying at speeds up to 1,000 miles per hour and at altitudes up to 60,000 feet, a guided missile of supersonic velocity should be developed. Range should be the maximum attainable, with 50,000 yards the present goal, and controllable maneuver of the missile should be sufficient to intercept an aircraft under those conditions.

    b. Interceptor Guided Missile. To intercept and destroy aircraft or V-2 type missiles traveling at very high altitudes at speeds greatly in excess of the sonic, there should be developed a guided missile of the greatest attainable velocity. It should have a range of at least 100,000

yards and possess the greatest accuracy of control and maneuverability commensurate with the speed of the missile. It should afford a high probability of destroying any aerial target coming within its operating range.

c. <u>Ground-to-Ground Short Range Guided Missile</u>. A guided missile should be developed to provide direct support to Army Ground Forces operations, including the reduction of fortifications and installations. Operating range up to 45,000 yards, accuracy at least equal to conventional artillery, and speed great enough to prevent its being engaged successfully by enemy armament, are desirable. It should be capable of employment within 2,000 yards of our own troops when equipped with a warhead of conventional explosives.

d. <u>Ground-to-Ground Long Range Guided Missile</u>. A missile is required for precision attacks on enemy ground installations at ranges up to at least 150 miles. It should have the maximum attainable destructive power for its size.

e. <u>Anti-Ship Guided Missile</u>. A guided missile is required to effect precision attacks on armored ships at ranges up to at least 150 miles. It should be capable of being guided or homed so as to effect a direct hit on a maneuvering naval vessel, hence should possess the maximum maneuverability and accuracy compatible with its speed, size, and range.

f. <u>Air-to-Ground Close Support Guided Missile</u>. An air-launched, air-to-ground guided missile for close support missions is needed. It should be self-propelled, capable of supersonic speed, and possess the maximum attainable accuracy and destructive effect.

g. <u>Ground-to-Ground Strategic Guided Missile</u>. There should be developed an exceptionally long range guided missile which can be employed at ranges of 150 to several thousand miles. It should be self-propelled at supersonic speed and have the maximum attainable accuracy and destructive effect. The warhead of this missile should be capable of carrying atomic explosive.

5. In view of the fact that so much basic research must be initiated and accomplished and that principles of design, once established for smaller missiles, may prove applicable to other types, careful study should be made to determine the types to be developed initially. Development of other types should be deferred until test models of these types have been completed. At that time, based upon experience obtained, the powers and limitations of guided missiles should be reviewed and firm requirements established as the basis for further development.

Considerations of Design

6. <u>Interchangeability</u>. It may be possible to design a single missile,

which, having interchangeable warheads (demolition, fragmentation, concrete or armor penetrating and chemical) will be suitable for ground-to-ground assault, anti-ship, and anti-submarine operations. The design of dual or multi-purpose missiles should be an ultimate objective. A choice of fuzing (VT, time, and remotely controllable) should be made available to facilitate interchangeability.

7. <u>Emplacement</u>. Guided missiles intended for tactical use, their associated warning, fire direction, fire control, and launching systems, should be designed to facilitate rapid emplacement and employment in the field. A minimum of time for preparation to launch, high launching rate, and quick removal from emplacement, are features required.

8. <u>Guiding Methods</u>. a. Guiding or homing systems should be free from mutual and enemy interference or countermeasures.

b. Provision for simultaneous control of a number of missiles launched at the same time, or in quick succession at the same or different targets, is desirable.

c. Guiding devices should be sufficiently sensitive and accurate to accomplish the missions of the several types of missiles. Research should investigate:

(1) A pre-set "memory" device such as self-contained compass, gyroscope and clockwork, with no external control after launching.

(2) The command system, consisting of observation of the missile by visual or electronic means and direction by radio control.

(3) Direction along a path, in which the missile follows an electronic beam.

(4) A homing device, incorporated within the missile, which seeks the target and then guides the missile by means of controllable surfaces.

9. <u>Methods of Propulsion</u>. Intensive research should be directed to provide efficient methods of propulsion. The rocket, turbo-jet, intermittent jet and ram-jet should be studied.

10. <u>Atomic Propulsion</u>. No means by which nuclear energy can be converted into thrust to propel a guided missile is foreseen for the near future. However, the increased effectiveness and range which would result from such development, together with the vast reduction in fuel weight of long range missiles, require a thorough investigation of this possibility.

CPSIA information can be obtained at www.ICGtesting.com
Printed in the USA
BVOW02s1207281014

372654BV00018B/518/P